MW01252949

THE SOCRATIC METHOD

Also available from Continuum:

Aristotle's Ethics, Hope May
Aristotle's Theory of Knowledge, Thomas Kiefer
Aristotle, Ethics and Pleasure, Michael Weinman
Cicero's Ethics, Harald Thorsrud
Happiness and Greek Ethical Thought, M. Andrew Holowchak
Plato's Stepping Stones, Michael Cormack
Stoic Ethics, William O. Stephens

16701

THE SOCRATIC METHOD

Plato's Use of Philosophical Drama

REBECCA BENSEN CAIN

GUELPH HUMBER LIBRARY
205 Humber College Blvd
Toronto, ON   M9W 5L7

continuum

Continuum International Publishing Group
The Tower Building, 11 York Road, London SE1 7NX
80 Maiden Lane, Suite 704, New York, NY 10038

© Rebecca Bensen Cain 2007

All rights reserved. No part of this publication may be reproduced or transmitted in
any form or by any means, electronic or mechanical, including photocopying, recording,
or any information storage or retrieval system, without prior permission in writing from
the publishers.

British Library Cataloguing-in-Publication Data
A catalogue record for this book is available from the British Library.

ISBN: HB: 0-8264-8891-9
        9780826488916

Library of Congress Cataloging-in-Publication Data
A catalog record for this book is available from the Library of Congress.

Typeset by Aarontype Limited, Easton, Bristol
Printed and bound in Great Britain by Biddles Ltd, King's Lynn, Norfolk

For Jim

Contents

Preface

The book is about Plato's use of drama in his dialogues and the philosophical method of Plato's Socrates. In my study of Plato, I am drawn inexorably to the idea that the way to read his dialogues is to read them as literature and as philosophy at the same time. I developed a great respect for the method of Socrates for several reasons which have to do mainly with self-education and self-knowledge. I came to realize both how nearly impossible it is to practice as a method of teaching and learning, and that there really is no way to teach or learn philosophy, other than to adopt some version of it.

Though I am not able, in this book, to give full reference to the long line of traditional thinkers who have written profoundly on Plato but have missed the limelight in Platonic studies, so to speak, I am indebted to all of them for teaching me how to read the dialogues. In writing the book, I have approached the secondary literature in Platonic scholarship gingerly so as not to get bogged down with issues that I would not be able to treat with adequate care and consideration. I do not give great attention to the many-headed problems of interpretation of the Platonic dialogues. My citations are intended mainly to be a useful guide to other works on the subjects I discuss. In citing sources, I have minimized commentary on what other authors have said in order to keep the book accessible and intelligible to the non-specialist reader. Since the book is the intellectual heir to my dissertation thesis (Bensen 1999) in which I have given copious notes and tireless care to the current issues that surround the topics of Plato and Socratic method, I am comfortable with having to forego much of the heavy weather now. I will refer the reader to the dissertation wherever this is appropriate.

I acknowledge my appreciation to the philosophy department at Oklahoma State University for having me as a member of their entourage. Above all, I wish to express personal gratitude to Jim, my husband, philosopher and confidant. The colleagues and professors who have helped to see me through my ideas are Voula Tsouna and Nick Smith, to whom I owe special thanks, and Herbert Garelick, Charles McCracken, Hubert

Schwyzer, Matthew Hanser and Richard Hall. I am grateful to the people at Continuum for their receptivity and support in producing the book, especially Jim Fieser, Philip de Bary, Adam Green, Sarah Douglas and Slav Todorov.

R.B.C.
June 2006

Abbreviations

Plato

Alc. I.	*Alcibiades I*
Ap.	*Apology*
Chrm.	*Charmides*
Cr.	*Crito*
Crat.	*Cratylus*
Eud.	*Euthydemus*
Eu.	*Euthyphro*
Grg.	*Gorgias*
HMaj.	*Hippias Major*
HMin.	*Hippias Minor*
La.	*Laches*
Ly.	*Lysis*
Men.	*Menexenus*
Parm.	*Parmenides*
Phd.	*Phaedo*
Phdr.	*Phaedrus*
Phil.	*Philebus*
Prt.	*Protagoras*
Rep.	*Republic*
Sym.	*Symposium*
Tht.	*Theaetetus*
Soph.	*Sophist*
St.	*Statesman*
Ti.	*Timaeus*

Aristotle

Metaph.	*Metaphysics*
NE	*Nicomachean Ethics*
Rh.	*Rhetoric*
SE	*Sophistici Elenchi*
Top.	*Topics*

Chapter 1

The Socratic Method of Dialectic

Introduction

In this study, I propose a psychological model of Socratic method (SM). I argue for this model in five ways. I claim that (i) the principal aim of the method is moral improvement through self-knowledge and there are three functions which serve this aim; (ii) the experience of *aporia*, the demand for sincerity, and the motivating effects of shame are the basic psychological features that contribute to self-knowledge; and (iii) the main presupposition on which the method rests is a claim about human nature: all humans, by nature, desire the good where 'good' is understood as happiness or that which conduces to happiness. This view is called 'psychological eudaimonism'. As part of the model, I offer a constructive interpretation of Socrates' moral position that involves two additional claims about his methodology: (iv) he makes use of regulative *endoxa*, the common or reputable opinions, as a dialectical strategy; and (v) he uses verbal ambiguity in his reinterpretation of the agreed-upon regulative endoxical premises. I show that the combined use of regulative endoxical premises and verbal ambiguity provides Socrates with a way to refute and to persuade the interlocutor, and gives him a basis for arguing for his own moral position as represented in the dialogues.

   This chapter is concerned with the first three claims and presents the moral-psychological features of the method. In explaining the psychological model, I attempt to clarify Socrates' moral aim, identify the three functions and discuss their relationship to the aim. I defend the moral aim briefly and discuss a number of critical questions that surround the topic of Socrates' practice of philosophy and Plato's dramatic presentation of the method. In the next chapter, I introduce the idea of regulative *endoxa*, which forms a part of claim (iv), and further discuss the three functions. I focus on the protreptic function and examine several versions of Socrates' protreptic style of argument taken from the texts.

I address claim (v) in Chapter 3, which begins with a discussion of the epistemic function and introduces the concept of ambiguity. I sort out the terminology that is relevant to the arguments and fallacies that Socrates constructs. Then I turn to key passages in the *Euthydemus* and *Protagoras* to explain the basic moves involved in the fallacy of equivocation. Next, I show how Socrates uses ambiguity based on his own moral and psychological beliefs to persuade the interlocutors to change their beliefs, desires and values, and to care above all about the soul and virtue. The refutations of Polemarchus in *Republic* I and Polus in the *Gorgias* are discussed at length.

The fourth chapter blends together the topics of ambiguity and drama in Plato and the ancient Greek literary tradition. The chapter provides historical background on ambiguity and fallacy in Aristotle and the Stoics and contrasts their approaches with the creative use of ambiguity. I suggest that a broader treatment of refutation and fallacy than is ordinarily presupposed is appropriate to the dialectical format in which Socrates and the Sophists operate and use their techniques. Developing the idea of the proper use of technique, I describe the relevant contrasts between SM and the methods of rhetoric used by the Sophists. Finally, I discuss Plato's use of drama in portraying the method. As part of my project I intend to show that Plato, as a philosopher and a dramatist-poet, is deeply concerned with the use and misuse of language and argumentation. His concerns are revealed in the dramatic context of the dialogues as well as in the arguments. His approach to the problems of language is revisionist; this revisionist approach is at the core of SM and it is expressed in the discourse of SM. Plato's art is everywhere in the dialogues and in SM. Plato's art is manifest through his use of poetic and dramatic elements to portray character and the psychological attributes of character in highly animated philosophical conversation. He builds these elements into the philosophical themes of the dialogues in a way that causes a fit between the logical and psychological components of SM.

The overall line of argument for the psychological interpretation of SM which I offer is this. There are five aspects of SM that must be included and explained in order to make the method intelligible and give it a justification it would not otherwise have. The first three show its moral purpose and psychological impact, and the last two show its logical and rhetorical underpinnings. These aspects cannot be explained unless the drama of the dialogues is taken fully into account. My interpretation gives the method an informal structure and motivational content. This content is grounded in the aim of moral self-improvement which is itself based on Socrates' psychological eudaimonism. On my reading of the dialogues, both Socrates as character and Plato as author believe that there is no such thing as a value-neutral method of inquiry into moral truths and the meaning of the good life. It seems to me that an appropriate way to begin a study of SM is with a concern for what motivates Socrates and how his moral and psychological beliefs support the method.

A Psychological Model

In the model, I propose three main dialectical activities of SM: refutation, truth-seeking and persuasion. The familiar Socratic *'elenchos'* identified with the refutation or cross-examination of interlocutors is considered to be only one function of the method which I call the 'elenctic' function. The Socratic search for knowledge, usually construed in terms of seeking definitions of the virtues by asking the 'what is it' question, I call the 'epistemic' function. The persuasive attempts that Socrates makes to lead the interlocutor toward a Socratic moral position, I call the 'protreptic' function. I argue that the protreptic function has a significant role to play in how Socrates constructs his elenctic arguments. What I mean by the word 'function' is that Socrates does something with the arguments he constructs; that is, he engages in argumentative modes of discourse which direct him towards his goal.

From the standpoint of this model, the term *'elenchos'* which is most commonly used to refer, either broadly or narrowly, to Socrates' method is not sufficient; it is confining and misleading. The term I use to refer generally to the method is 'dialectic' which at its most fundamental level means 'conversation', 'talk' or 'discourse'. To define SM broadly as a dialectical method is to regard it as a philosophical conversation or discussion which proceeds by question and answer. In referring to SM in the strict sense, I use the phrase 'Socratic dialectic' to mean Socrates' method of reasoned inquiry, in the form of a philosophical conversation usually between two people, conducted through question and answer, and structured by the goal of moral self-improvement.[1]

In the grandest outline, to study SM is to study the nature of dialectic in the form that is most pervasive in the Platonic corpus, even as it is transformed into what is called 'Platonic method' or 'Platonic dialectic'. What I mean here is that the discursive features of SM are still identifiable within other conceptions of dialectic which Plato uses in the 'middle' and 'later' dialogues. In the cumulative body of Plato's works, SM becomes part of newer structures and modes of inquiry, such as the method of hypothesis introduced in the *Meno*. SM evolves into a composite methodology which includes the 'second-best' method used in the *Phaedo* that follows upon

Socrates' narrative of his changing point of view. A distinctively metaphysical and Platonic method of hypothesis through dialectic is offered in
the *Republic*; this is the method by which philosophers are able to know the
Forms which culminates in a vision of the Form of the Good. Socrates says
that he would 'give the name dialectician to the man who is able to exact an
account of the essence of each thing' (534b).[2] And finally, there is the
method of collection and division introduced in the *Phaedrus*, and developed
in the *Philebus*, *Statesman* and *Sophist*.

As a discursive method of reasoning, SM has limitations which are intrin-
sic to its specific form, normative content and scope. Broader boundaries are
set by the dramatic elements created by Plato as the author. Plato casts the
character of Socrates as the protagonist or philosophical hero, and
he is set on a stage with a host of characters who are his interlocutors with
their assigned roles to play. The silent presence of the audience of listeners
and by standers from within the dramatic context puts a literary frame
around the dialogues. Add to this mix Plato's readership of a given time
period and the multiple perspectives provided by generations of inter-
preters, and the delightful result is two distinct layers of meaning from
which to discuss Socratic argumentation in the dialogues. One may look at
Socrates' speech, his way of conducting himself and how he treats his interlocutors from the internal perspective of the dramatic action and characterization, and become fully engaged with the arguments on this level, or one
may pull back and look at the dramas from the external, textual perspective
in which Plato, the author, communicates with his readers.

It is necessary and important for the purposes of this study to recognize
that interpreting the dialogues as dramatic, artistically bound texts enables
a reader to make fruitful use of both perspectives or layers of meaning.
Hence, I distinguish between two frames or orders of reading the dialogues:
the first-order reading I refer to as the 'internal frame' or 'dramatic level',
and the second-order reading I refer to as the 'textual frame' or 'literary
level'. As readers, we may engage ourselves at either level or on both at the
same time. Once we step beyond the internal frame of the dialogue and
recognize the hermeneutic aspects of the Platonic text, it will be possible to
consider what Socrates says and does as involving us in Plato's literary purposes, his critical motivations, his artistic creativity and resourcefulness of
imagination, and his magical play of language. Outside of the internal
frame, it will be easier for readers to see how we are involved as students of
Plato and become a part of his pedagogical intentions. This distinction will
facilitate my efforts to explain and justify the complex psycho-dynamics
of SM. As readers we are members of Socrates' and Plato's audiences.
We listen to Socrates speak and we read Plato. As listeners, we judge the

interactions, speeches and arguments from within the internal frame of the dialectic and we are expected to question the value of SM; we will want to know what benefits the method has and what harm it incurs. As readers of Plato's text, we may criticize or praise a dialogue for its literary style, dramatic composition and formal structure, its use of imagery, the presentation of characters, and for the philosophical depth and the levels of meaning it offers.

There are context-sensitive features which fill in the drama of Socrates as dialectician practicing his art. Such features are the historical background which infuses the dialogue and its characters with a situation, the attitude of a specific interlocutor and the attending psychological factors, for example the desire to compete and win, and feelings of pride, shame, confusion, contempt, frustration, impatience and anger, all of which clearly affect the force and the direction of the argumentation Socrates uses. The recognition that these contextual aspects are squarely within the dialectical context rather than extraneous to it, and that the dialectical context is part of the dramatic world of Plato, is central to my interpretation. The specific attention given to how these aspects fit into a particular dialogue constitutes one of the major differences between the psychological approach to SM which I adopt and the standard models based on an epistemological approach.

What I call the 'epistemological model' of SM focuses on Socrates' philosophical views conceived in terms of his search for moral knowledge through definitions. The dialogues are mainly interpreted as sources of Socratic or Platonic doctrine. Philosophical problems about what Socrates knows or believes, and how he establishes or fails to establish certain moral truths associated with Socratic ethics, are pursued through logical analysis of propositions and arguments. Broadly speaking, such models are represented by the works of Richard Robinson, Gregory Vlastos, Gerasimos Santas and Terence Irwin who offer a logic-centered, doctrinal analysis of methodology in Socrates' and Plato's thought.[3] My approach will contrast strongly with these authors and with several prominent scholars who write on the topic of SM.[4] These scholars, while critical of the views of the aforementioned authors, belong to the doctrinal or analytic tradition and adopt a similar framework of assumptions.[5]

Vlastos' Epistemological Model

Before I present the psychological model of SM, I give some initial consideration to the view put forth by Gregory Vlastos, whose influence on all matters concerning the Platonic Socrates is inexhaustible.[6] Vlastos identifies

SM with the Socratic practice of cross-examination known as the *elenchos*. The *elenchos* is identified with a logical device Socrates uses for refuting the interlocutor by testing his alleged knowledge, or a set of beliefs, for consistency. The interlocutor puts forward a thesis that he thinks is true. By means of a series of questions and answers, Socrates is able to draw the opposite conclusion of the interlocutor's thesis from premises the interlocutor accepts. With this formal procedure in mind, Vlastos defines the Socratic *elenchos* as 'a search for moral truth by adversary argument in which a thesis is debated only if asserted as the answerer's own belief, who is regarded as refuted if and only if the negation of his thesis is deduced from his own beliefs'.[7]

According to Vlastos, the goal of the *elenchos* is moral knowledge; it is pursued primarily through the search for the essential nature, or true definition, of virtue. As I interpret Vlastos' model, his analysis focuses almost exclusively on the epistemic function of SM. Vlastos is concerned with how Socrates gets at the truths he seeks, what conceptions of truth are operating, what kind of knowledge Socrates has, what kind of knowledge Socrates lacks and what methods he uses to justify his own beliefs. Socrates' method is regarded as a 'search for moral truth' by means of the elenctic arguments which refute the various theses of Socrates' interlocutors in Plato's 'early' group of dialogues. Vlastos' view of the *elenchos* is called 'constructivist' since he sees the elenctic arguments as yielding positive results from which Socrates' moral views can be derived.[8] He rejects those views of the Socratic *elenchos* which construe it purely as a negative method for falsifying or destroying the interlocutor's thesis, and removing the interlocutor's conceit of wisdom.[9] Rather, Vlastos argues that Socrates seeks to discover and establish the truth by means of the *elenchos*.

Vlastos does acknowledge that the *elenchos* is 'pervasively negative in form', but its form contrasts sharply with the content of Socrates' aim which, he claims, is 'strongly positive: to discover and defend true moral doctrine'.[10] I agree with Vlastos that SM is constructive and seeks to know truth, but this truth-seeking activity is extremely indirect and subject to the qualifications placed on it by the conversational format of the argumentation. Socrates' way of searching for the truth is by means of a 'joint inquiry' (*koinē skepsis*).[11] His method is influenced by a moral ideal of human goodness which is inspired by a conception of divine wisdom. Because the meaning of truth is directed by a moral ideal, the truth-seeking activity is a normative function and not the goal of the method. To say that it is a 'normative' function means that it serves to improve others morally simply by engaging in this activity. The truth-seeking activities, though they involve both inductive and deductive forms of reasoning, do not serve to establish

truth directly through demonstration from true premises and first principles. Socrates does search for a true account of virtue and the search is
grounded on rational principles and definitions which regulate the activities. However, by defining the primary objective of SM in terms of 'true
moral doctrine' and treating such doctrine as the conclusions of deductively
valid arguments, Vlastos has formalized and simplified an informal and
multi-dimensional method.

The dialectical context for the truth-seeking activities relies on an
exchange between two people and what can be agreed between them, and
this indicates the need to limit the meaning of what it is to arrive at the truth
of a conclusion deductively. In its truth-seeking function, the method starts
out with some common agreement about what is true. Socrates is concerned
with how the interlocutor stands in relation to the truth of his own beliefs
and the search for truth is governed, to a large extent, by what he is willing
to admit given the topic at hand. In light of this qualification, the truth-seeking activity is part of a dialectical method which includes both elenctic and
protreptic functions. The protreptic function is involved in the Socratic process of interpreting what the truth of a belief means, and what it implies for
the interlocutor, as well as for Socrates.

Given that Socrates constructs elenctic arguments as a means of testing
the interlocutor's thesis for its truth value, Vlastos' interpretation generates
a problem which he calls the 'problem of the *elenchos*'.[12] This is the problem
of how a method which tests only for consistency between an interlocutor's
beliefs can discover moral truth. The problem poses an interpretive obstacle
for the constructivist view which holds that there is a definitive moral position to be attributed to Socrates in the 'early' dialogues. If the *elenchos* tests
only for consistency and there is no other independent means by which
Socrates arrives at his positive moral principles, then it is difficult to figure
out how Socrates grounded his beliefs and is so convinced of their truth. This
is a puzzle which Vlastos poses and tries to solve. His solution to the problem
attributes an epistemological assumption to SM that is implausibly strong,
and requires that Socrates use only true premises in the elenctic arguments
he constructs. However, the texts show Socrates relying upon premises
which he appears not to accept, working from the truth of ordinary conventional opinions (*endoxa*), and using faulty logical reasoning in the elenctic
arguments. Hence, Vlastos has not been successful in resolving the issues
which his 'problem of the *elenchos*' has raised.

Vlastos' account of the *elenchos* and the critical responses to his views constitute an enormous amount of the scholarly literature on the topic of SM.
His position covers many topics in Platonic scholarship and it is too complex
to be managed within this study. I am concerned with only a small part of

the package Vlastos offers. With respect to the constructivist side of his approach which involves how to derive the positive results of the Socratic moral position from elenctic arguments, I believe that Socrates' position cannot be properly assessed through Vlastos' model because it relies upon an interpretive approach which de-contextualizes passages and isolates the elenctic arguments from the dialectical context of the dialogues.

The elenctic arguments by themselves cannot provide a direct source for the assessment of Socrates' moral position because they are constructed from the beliefs of the interlocutor and geared to his specific character. Moreover, the elenctic arguments are enmeshed within the drama that Plato creates. The Platonic dialogue is a unified collaboration of philosophical and literary elements which makes the argumentation and the interaction between the participants all the more exciting and realistic. The contextual features of the dialectical exchanges are not drawbacks but an aesthetic advantage for the interpreter who seeks to understand how SM operates.

The personal and particular aspects that infuse the dialogues give the SM its unique '*ad hominem*' and existential dimensions. The *ad hominem* aspects involve the specific attributes of the character of the interlocutor who feels the pressure of being questioned and is forced to express his beliefs openly in public. The interlocutor may think he is being personally challenged or attacked and the argumentation targets his interests and emotional reactions. The three psychological components, *aporia*, the sincerity demand and shame, are the *ad hominem* effects of SM. In general, the existential dimension refers to the fact that the questions that Socrates poses to the interlocutor are directly concerned with how he lives his life. As I interpret the existential import of SM with regard to the dialectical context, it means that the interlocutor is faced with a choice, in the dramatic moment, about what to believe and what standpoint he will take. Socrates' method of dialectic is inherently critical about whatever views are at issue, whether they purportedly belong to Socrates, or the particular interlocutor, or to the poets, or the Athenian majority, the *dēmos*. If Socrates has done his job properly, it will not be possible to extract from the elenctic arguments Socrates' own beliefs as conclusions generated from the premises of such arguments.

The Moral Aim

The first step in explaining the psychological model of SM is to clarify Socrates' moral aim. Socrates is interested in moral truth and the method can be understood initially as an inquiry into moral truth, but Socrates' search for wisdom should not be interpreted in a deductive framework which conceives of argumentation as simply a way to prove true conclusions from true premises. In my interpretation, to say that Socrates aims at moral truth is to say that his method has a function of seeking the truth indirectly through dialogue with others, using their assumptions, agreements and inferences based on their moral beliefs and social values. The subjects of inquiry about which Socrates seeks to know the truth with his interlocutors are simultaneously philosophical/theoretical and personal/practical; they have everything to do with how each of us is to become a better human being.

Socrates is sometimes very explicit about his motive in questioning others, which is that he always aims at the good of the souls of whomever he meets and at his own good (*Chrm.* 166c-e; *Grg.* 505e; *Prt.* 348c-e). Of course, the emphasis on the 'soul' (*psuchē*) of the interlocutor puts an entirely different perspective on the meaning of the 'good' as the object of desire which he aims to bring about. This point of emphasis concerns the kind of moral benefit that Socrates takes himself to be offering and will be discussed later. For the present, it should be noted that there exists an enormous potential for ambiguity and miscommunication between Socrates and his interlocutors, with regard to ordinary usage and the conventional meaning of pairs of terms such as good/bad and beneficial/harmful which the interlocutor will assume, and the meaning which Socrates will assign to these terms. As I hope to show later in this study, Socrates will often initially go along with the interlocutor and sometimes assume the interlocutor's conventional meaning of good, when it suits the argument he wishes to make, and sometimes he will assume his own special, Socratic meaning of 'good' as 'morally good' or 'good for the soul'.

The aim of SM is moral improvement as it pertains to Socrates himself and to his interlocutors, but more needs to be said about the role of the interlocutor because the way in which Socrates hopes to improve the interlocutor morally has to do with Socrates' concept of self-knowledge. Improving the interlocutor morally through self-knowledge means that the interlocutor must take the initiative to improve himself, and that the improvement takes place psychologically within the interlocutor's soul, which for the time being may be understood broadly in terms of the mental life of the interlocutor: his beliefs, emotions, and desires. The moral aim of the method both explains and justifies the personal, or *ad hominem*, nature of the elenctic function and the particularized, subjective nature of the truth-seeking function. If Socrates always attempts to make the interlocutor a better man, then he must tend to the individual needs of the interlocutor's soul and construct the argument accordingly. SM is not simply a method of reasoned argument, but a method of constructing an argument to refute and persuade an interlocutor with an individual personality. The emphasis on the personal dimension of doing philosophy through dialectic restores the proper meaning to the method as an inquiry into moral truth that mutually affects the questioner and the answerer, and aims to benefit both.

Examples from the Texts

The controversy over whether Socrates, as he is presented in Plato's dialogues, corrupts or improves his associates is a central question which any account of SM must address. It is the premier concern of the *Apology*, given the political nature of Socrates' practice, the negative image of the intellectual given to him by Aristophanes in the comedy, *Clouds*, and the notorious reputations of his former associates, Critias and Alcibiades. None the less, Plato dramatizes Socrates' integrity; he is unwavering in his own opinion about the benefits of refutation and philosophical inquiry. When examining Meletus, Socrates takes the line of reasoning that no one would ever knowingly corrupt his associates, for to do so would be to harm oneself (25e–26b). In defending his activities, he says that he has devoted himself to conferring upon each man individually 'what I say is the greatest benefit, by trying to persuade him not to care for any of his belongings before caring that he should be as good and as wise as possible' (36c5–6, trans. Grube). And he declares that 'the greatest good for a man is to discuss virtue every day' (38a3–4). With characteristically shameless arrogance from the point of view of his fellow Athenians, Socrates compares himself to Achilles and to an Olympian victor. He tells the jury, 'The Olympian victor makes you think yourself happy; I make you be happy' (36e1).

He believes that being cross-examined is a great service because it is through this activity that one can learn to recognize one's ignorance. In order to learn about one's ignorance, one must first find out what one believes. This is mainly the way that the elenctic function of the method facilitates self-knowledge. The elenctic function is beneficial because it roots out a special type of self-deception or self-ignorance. In the *Protagoras*, Socrates is questioning the Sophists as a group, about the meaning of moral weakness which had just been explained as doing what is worse contrary to what one knows (or believes) is better. Moral weakness is caused by self-ignorance, where 'ignorance' is 'having a false belief and being deceived about matters of importance' (*peri tōn pragmatōn tōn pollou axiōn*; 358c7–9).

In the *Euthydemus*, Socrates urges Cleinias to submit himself to the eristic Sophist, Euthydemus, for questioning and says, 'Have no fear, Cleinias; answer bravely, whichever you think it is: for perchance he is doing you the greatest service in the world' (275d10-e2). Socrates assures Gorgias that he does not mind being refuted and that it is better than refuting, 'insofar as it is a greater good to be rid of the greatest evil from oneself than to rid someone else of it. I don't suppose that any evil for a man is as great as false belief about the things we're discussing right now' (*Grg.* 458a-b, trans. Zeyl). In the *Hippias Minor*, Socrates asks Hippias to help him figure out whether it is better to err voluntarily or involuntarily, and tells him, 'for you will be doing me much more good if you cure my soul of ignorance, than if you were to cure my body of disease' (372e). Later, in the *Euthydemus*, Socrates tells Ctessipus that he is willing to allow Dionysodorus 'to do to me whatever he pleases: only he must make me good' (285c7).

Clearly Socrates believes that SM improves the interlocutor's soul but it takes only a reading of a few dialogues for a reader to wonder whether SM is truly beneficial and whether Socrates succeeds or fails with his interlocutors. It is part of my project to address these questions. The project is a self-reflexive one because Plato asks the reader to rethink the meanings of benefit/harm and success/failure in light of what Socrates says and does. With particular regard to the elenctic function, I argue that benefits and harms cannot be adequately explained or appreciated without consideration of the protreptic function and how it works with the elenctic function to achieve the moral aim. Regarding the moral aim, Socrates thinks that whatever a person does is done, and should be done consciously, for the sake of the good (*Grg.* 499e-500a). His aim is expressed by a teleological principle of morality known as 'moral eudaimonism'. This principle holds that the aim of all action is happiness and that an action gets its value from the intention of the agent and the ends which the action serves (*Grg.* 467c-468e; *La.* 185a-186c; *Ly.* 219c-220b). Throughout the dialogues, Socrates focuses on the soul of the interlocutor, directs his questioning towards the product or *ergon* of an activity in order to explain its value, and is explicitly concerned with making others as good as possible.[13]

A dialogue that dramatizes Socrates' moral/psychological eudaimonism and its relation to his protreptic discourse is the *Euthydemus*. Socrates requests that the eristic brothers display their talents by persuading the young Cleinias to pursue wisdom and virtue since they agree that it is by the same art that one can teach virtue and persuade others to learn it. Cleinias is at the delicate age of being impressionable and could easily be corrupted or improved by his associates. Socrates says, 'I and all of us here are at this moment anxious for him to become as good as possible'

(275a8-9). After giving his own protreptic speech (*protreptikon logon*: 282d9) as an example for the brothers to follow, Socrates emphasizes the point again and says 'it really is a matter of great moment to us that this youth should become wise and good' (282e10-283a1).

Overview of the Three Functions

In this section, I introduce the three modes of discourse of SM briefly with respect to Socrates' moral purposes. In Chapter 2, I discuss these modes or dialectical functions in connection with Socratic argumentation and develop these connections. Socrates' goal of moral self-improvement is what ultimately justifies his method and the means he uses for educating the interlocutor. His means is rational discourse and argumentation, and the education is a therapeutic process of making an individual philosophically self-aware, that is to say, the individual becomes aware of his self-ignorance and his psychological or moral inconsistencies. Socrates is always in the mode of dialectical discourse, and while each mode has a specific function and immediate aim, all three modes of discourse, refutation, truth-seeking and persuasion contribute to the ultimate goal of self-knowledge. Any increase in self-knowledge is moral improvement because it increases the interlocutor's chances for understanding virtue and human goodness in himself and others. Each function serves the aim in a different way. The epistemic function provides the impetus for Socratic dialectic to begin. It was introduced as part of the critical discussion of Vlastos' epistemological model.

The elenctic function occurs as soon as Socrates critically examines the interlocutor's beliefs for inconsistency. Socrates engages the interlocutor in the activities of expressing his beliefs, recognizing his own ignorance, figuring out why he was refuted, discovering the meaning of the concepts he uses and realizing what premises he is ultimately committed to in making his moral judgments. With the persuasive or protreptic function, Socrates hopes to persuade the interlocutor to care for his soul by engaging in philosophical activity, and seeking the wisdom that he lacks. Socrates works to reorientate the interlocutor's value system. He does this directly by exhortation and protreptic argumentation. He also does this indirectly, by means of elenctic argumentation which allows him the opportunity to replace the interlocutor's false beliefs with true beliefs through conceptual revision.

A major part of my thesis is to argue that Socrates uses ambiguity, in the interpretive process of constructing an argument, and show how he attempts to change the meaning of the beliefs the interlocutor already has by conceptual reorientation. I shall argue that placing the proper emphasis on the protreptic function is the best explanation of Socrates' use of ambiguity, and his corresponding attempt to find common ground on which to base his arguments. In order to change the way the interlocutor perceives his moral experience, Socrates draws upon that experience, and explores the ambiguities of the language which the interlocutor uses to describe it.

The elenctic and protreptic functions require that the interlocutor know himself better than he does. These activities are 'self-educating' because they are ways of educating the soul without the authority of a moral expert. Socrates is not a moral expert; he denies having any knowledge of virtue, and does not 'teach' in any conventional sense of the term. The dialectical functions provide the grounds for the educational activities; however, it is up to the particular interlocutor to decide whether, and to what extent, he will participate in them. Specifically, the interlocutor must play an active role by stating his beliefs clearly and distinguishing between meanings of the terms and concepts. The elenctic and protreptic functions of the SM make strong demands on the interlocutor's intellect and require a considerable amount of independent initiative and careful thinking from the interlocutor, if he is to improve himself morally.

The method and its moral aim, as I've described it so far, are subject to the objection that it is imprecise, open-ended and too flexible, allowing just about any dialectical practices or policies to be followed as long as they can be described as fitting under the Socratic rubric of increasing self-knowledge, benefiting his interlocutors and himself in the process. For instance, Socrates' elenctic discourse involves an ungracious style of questioning that forces the interlocutor into a corner, trapping him with a net of wordy questions and then pushing him to answer truthfully, as if this kind of pressure tactic lends itself to an honest response on the interlocutor's part.

Related to this pressure tactic is Socrates' habit of imposing himself upon the interlocutor in the name of truth and mutual inquiry, when he is clearly moving his agenda forward rather than drawing out the interlocutor's considered opinions and actually securing a genuine agreement. The pressure tactics are offensive; they frequently have a negative effect on the interlocutors and probably alienate the observers, as well as making many of Plato's readers cringe. The negative impact of the method has a psychological and a logical dimension and both dimensions pose problems for appreciating SM.

The Moral Aim Defended

The personal dimension, quick adaptability and lofty moral intentions which I attribute to SM will clash with what many readers find upon examining Socrates' practice in the dialogues. At first sight, Socrates appears to be an unassuming, flexible and sincere person, but as it often turns out, he shows himself to be uncompromising, harsh and ironically sincere. In developing the psychological model, there will be a self-imposed demand to defend Socrates' dialectical tactics in light of his moral aim to benefit himself and others. I attempt to meet this demand with a justificatory approach that is divided into two types. One type is the 'Socratic' justification which belongs to the internal frame reading of the dialogues as dramas. It situates Socrates as a philosopher with a moral purpose, in a specific setting, with a certain set of characters within a given dialogue.

The other type is the 'Platonic' justification. It derives from the reader taking Plato's literary purposes fully into account and letting the possible reasons he has for writing the dialogues form a meaningful part of one's interpretation of SM. Plato's use of dramatic contexts and multiple perspectives in presenting Socrates' character and method provides an assortment of philosophical themes and standpoints which suggest moral, aesthetic, theoretical and pedagogical reasons for writing the dialogues. Looking at SM from Plato's authorial perspective broadens the reader's appreciation of the skill with which Plato adopts numerous styles and themes from Greek tragic and comic poetry and puts their techniques to philosophical uses. For example, the narrative style Socrates exemplifies when he tells the myth of the water carriers using etymological puns (*Grg.* 493a-494a) is similar to the style of speech given by Tiresias in Euripides' *Bacchae* (272-97).[14] By means of these techniques, he achieves a critical distance from the arguments and attitudes of the characters, including Socrates; the authorial standpoint also absolves Plato of any personal responsibility for the dialectical misconduct, pretenses, and paradoxical views wrought well by the various *personae* of Socrates.

To some extent, the Socratic justification relies on the personal and moral character of Socrates, his *ēthos*. There is an urgency that Socrates apparently feels and exhibits in confronting the ordinary Athenian's conventional morality which supports a tradition that he finds dangerous and harmful. As Plato's readers, we ought to respect the personal commitment Socrates makes to change Athenian educational practices and bring about moral reform and understand the significance of Socrates' conception of philosophy as rooted in truth, wisdom and virtue in contrast to the worldly advice and teachings of the sophistic and rhetorical tradition of his day. Socrates is being presented in strong opposition both to the conventional norms of his culture and to the Sophists who represent the new education (*paideia*). The best approach towards SM is one that takes into account the dramatic picture that Plato draws for us in all of its details. It is a picture that localizes the character and critical role of Socrates as a philosopher in Athenian society at a politically tumultuous time and place. I suggest that this attitude has the best chance of making sense of Socrates' moral character, his conduct and his argumentation.

The reader needs to put great trust in the complicatedly rich portrait of the character of Socrates as Plato presents him in the dialogues. A. A. Long makes an interesting case for what he calls the 'plasticity of Plato's Socrates'.[15] Long argues that the many-sidedness of Socrates, and the range of portraits which Plato offers his readers, make it possible for Plato to develop Socrates and his methodology in progressively new ways. This plasticity provides Plato with an all-purpose philosophical medium with which to project the moral character of Socrates and defend his way of life. The Socratic/Platonic justification I offer appeals to the idea of Socrates as a chameleon philosopher who changes with each dialogue but remains somehow the same. He is presented as an elenctic gadfly, a rhetorician, sophist, philosopher-therapist or midwife, as Erōs, as an ironist, a religious seeker, an intellectualist, a moral reformer and a true educator. In every case, Socrates is portrayed as the dialectician, but with many faces, who can be disguised, molded and modified to fit different contexts and express a variety of views. Readers may react to the plurality of images in untold ways. For instance, if one feels that Socrates is overbearing, hubristic, fickle or elusive, he is like the god, Erōs; he has a great passion inside of him and he attracts all types, many of whom he could not possibly convert to philosophy. If one thinks that he is nurturing or paternalistic, he is a doctor or therapist who cares too much for his patients and thinks it is his job to administer painful psychological medicine. As a midwife, he is barren but gentle and encouraging; as a gadfly, he is petty and bothersome; as an ironist, he is mocking and bitter or acts like a fool; as an intellectualist, he puts too much stock in reason; as a religious figure he puts too much faith in the gods or the rewards of an afterlife.

In any case, it is all too obvious to readers who are sympathetic to the moral aim of the Platonic Socrates that the majority of citizens in democratic Athens did not believe that the historical Socrates made his associates morally better. Given the picture that Plato offers of his Socrates as a moral reformer who never misses an opportunity to say over and over again whatever he believed would make his fellow citizens better human beings, it is not at all surprising that he was a constant source of irritation and misunderstanding to his own community. This critical theme will be one amongst several striking ironic elements that contribute to the dramatic scenes that Plato presents to his readers.

Historically, there has been an abundance of favorable and unfavorable responses to Socrates' character and method comprising an interesting backlog of criticism dating from his fellow Athenian citizens and a barrage of humorous attacks by Aristophanes, the comedian, who satirized Socrates as a foolish quack in *The Clouds* to the bitter condemnations of Nietzsche, in the *Twilight of the Idols*, who vilifies Socrates' rationalism as decadent and deceptive. From within Plato's dialogues, there is Callicles and Thrasymachus who consider Socrates to be a pettifogger and openly question his motives, and Alcibiades who lashes out at Socrates for rejecting his erotic advances and accuses Socrates of hubris. The criticisms brought by Clitophon in the short dialogue named after him, though not attributed to Plato, reflect an important challenge to Socrates' form of protreptic discourse.

In the next section, I discuss three psychological elements that contribute to the *ad hominem* aspect of SM. One is the experience of *aporia*, the second is the demand for sincerity which generates the psycho-dynamics between Socrates and the interlocutor, and raises the issue of integrity. The third element is the feeling of shame that often accompanies the elenctic discourse. Broadly speaking, shame is a kind of fear of the negative opinions of others. All three elements target the interlocutor's sense of himself at the most personal level; they force him to confront his weaknesses and reflect on his commitments. If the interlocutor does not express himself truthfully due to shame or a lack of integrity, it may thwart the elenctic arguments, but the process reveals the interlocutor to himself, none the less.

Aporia and its Psychological Effects

In general, elenctic arguments are constructed by the questioner to refute the answerer by getting him to contradict himself. In Socratic dialectic, the immediate purpose of the refutation is to induce the experience of *aporia* in the interlocutor and cause him to wonder why he is confounded and perplexed about those things which he took himself to know so well. The Greek term '*aporia*' translates in English as 'difficulty', 'perplexity', 'without resources', or 'being at a loss'.[16] The term may be applied in two ways that are related to each other. The first has to do with the internal frame and state of mind of the interlocutor. Socrates tries to bring about *aporia* as quickly and directly as possible, so that the interlocutor will be ready for philosophical inquiry. From the interlocutor's point of view, however, the experience is negative: he has been silenced and defeated and does not know why. He may withdraw, ask Socrates for help or blame Socrates for bewitching him. Socrates sometimes tries to avoid negative reactions and may reassure the interlocutor that he is not under attack, but this is hardly enough to make a difference in the outcome, for an interlocutor who is refuted rarely feels that he has been treated justly.[17] In the drama of the dialogue, if an interlocutor admits his ignorance openly, a definite stage in the progress of SM is marked (*Chrm.* 162b-c; *Cr.* 50a; *La.* 194a-c; 196b-c, *Rep.* I 334b).

The term is also applied to the end of a Platonic dialogue, in which case, '*aporia*' refers to an apparently failed inquiry. To call a dialogue 'aporetic' indicates that no positive solution to the search for a definition, or other answers to Socratic questions, have been found.[18] This type of *aporia* has significance for the relationship between Plato and his reader. The reader who expects to find a solution to the problems Plato raises in the dialogue is left without an answer and might feel at a loss. The total effect of such dialogues is ambiguous. The endings allow for multiple interpretations of what has been settled or achieved and many questions are left open for readers to reflect on and decide for themselves. It is not certain what Plato intends his readers to understand from the unresolved endings, but it is likely that he wants his readers to feel something like the kind of *aporia* the interlocutors felt in the drama. Clearly, Plato hopes to prevent readers from thinking that there are formulaic answers to questions about virtue and the meaning of happiness which could be summed up in a few parting words of wisdom from Socrates.

Aporia and the Elenctic Function

In a refutation, there is usually a series of five identifiable stages. Socrates must get the interlocutor to formulate an initial statement or thesis which is then offered up for examination. In this initial stage, Socrates gives some direction and encouragement to the interlocutor. In cases where a specific definition is requested, Socrates provides some basic criteria, as in the *Euthyphro*, or an example of what he's looking for, as in the *Meno*. Often, since the precise meaning of the initial thesis or the subsequent theses is unclear as formulated, Socrates revises the thesis in his own words and puts it up for acceptance by the interlocutor. When the interlocutor accepts it, the thesis can be said, but only loosely said, to have been proposed or asserted by the interlocutor.

The second stage of the refutation mainly consists of Socrates trying to get the interlocutor to agree on a set of premises that may or may not seem related to the original thesis. Once the interlocutor agrees to the premises, where these premises entail the opposite of his thesis, the interlocutor is stuck in a contradiction, and experiences *aporia* which is an indication of his ignorance. The occurrence of *aporia* marks a third stage, and a formal turning point in the process of moral inquiry because it testifies to the fact that the interlocutor is ignorant and this ignorance puts him on the same epistemic level as Socrates with regard to the truth about the subject matter. The interlocutor naturally resists the feeling of *aporia* and rarely does he grant that his ignorance has been shown. Yet, the fact remains that the interlocutor contradicted himself by his own agreements and did not know how to defend himself against the refutation. This turning point in the dialectic marks a fourth stage which may be either subtly or noticeably constructive, depending on the dialogue. A shift in the action and the discourse occurs, which has Socrates taking the lead in the discussion and showing the interlocutor, albeit indirectly, a possible way out of the impasse. Frequently, a fifth and final stage occurs. Socrates may deliberately obscure the positive content he has offered, or the interlocutor may fail to follow, or something else serves to throw the dialectic back into *aporia*.

If the interlocutor allows himself to feel the effects of *aporia*, he becomes effectively aware of his ignorance. This awareness draws his attention inward and makes him reflect on his beliefs and the limitations of his knowledge. If the beliefs that the interlocutor expressed are genuine and represent his real values, as in the cases of Laches, Lysis, Polemarchus, Theaetetus, Simmias and Cebes, he is perplexed and tries to figure out what has gone wrong. If the interlocutor's reputation is at stake, as in the cases of Hippias, Gorgias, Polus and Protagoras, he associates *aporia* with defeat and shame. If the interlocutor thinks he has been tricked, he feels anger and blames Socrates as Callicles and Thrasymachus do. In any case, the experience of *aporia* makes the interlocutor feel uncomfortable, and some interlocutors will do whatever they can to avoid it.[19] The occurrence of *aporia*, or the obvious refusal to admit the experience, is a standard feature of SM.

Sincerity and Integrity

The demand for sincerity in dialectic requires that the interlocutor be honest about what his beliefs actually are and that he agree only to premises which he truly accepts.[20] Socrates depends on the interlocutor's sincerity because it is the only way that the method will have the personal effects on the interlocutor that Socrates intends it to have.[21] Clearly the interlocutor must stand behind what he says if the elenctic argument Socrates constructs to refute him is to have any therapeutic value or persuasive force. Further, to assert what one sincerely believes entails that one is willing to act upon the belief. Underlying the relation between a person's actions and beliefs, as represented by their speech, is a person's moral integrity.

Sincerity in speech is always preferred and expected but it is not absolutely demanded. Socrates tries to set dialectical standards but these are allowed to bend, as the drama illustrates in the *Protagoras* (331b-d), *Gorgias* (497a-c) and *Republic* I (346a-b). Socrates is able to deal with interlocutors who are unwilling to be sincere. Sincerity connotes that one ought to mean what one says. A person who lacks sincerity in his speech gives himself away whether he wants to or not, for sincerity indicates integrity or the lack thereof. Integrity connotes that a person is willing to do what he says and not hesitate to act upon his values and beliefs. Both sincerity and integrity depend upon the interlocutor's ability to understand how his beliefs are related to each other and to his actions. This kind of understanding results from actively engaging in dialectic and is a form of self-knowledge. So, in SM, there is not just a 'saying-believing' criterion at work but a 'saying-doing' criterion as well.

Vlastos takes note of the way in which the *elenchos* tests lives and not merely propositions and he refers to this as the 'existential dimension' of SM.[22] But his account of the nature of sincerity as an existential demand on the interlocutor is limited due to his concern with the formal methodology of the *elenchos* rather than with the dialectical method as it is shown through the drama and its psychology. What I understand by the 'existential' dimension of SM is that the interlocutor must choose at a given moment which way he will go in answering Socrates' questions. Either way he chooses, whether he will be sincere in his responses to Socrates or not, reveals his moral character.

There is a notable difference between testing for sincerity in terms of logical consistency which is expressed by a given proposition and its negation, and testing for sincerity as a sign of integrity. The most important way that one can show one's commitment to the truth of a belief is if one is willing to act upon it. How else can Plato show us this aspect of SM except through the details of the drama: the characters interacting in the conversation? What makes a belief more than a mere proposition is that the belief can be expressed in other ways. In literature this happens through character portrayal, and in Plato's dialogues it is conveyed also by the dramatization of SM.

Examples from the Texts

Both Nicias and Laches make the same point, in different ways, about the psychological impact of SM. Nicias' comments are often quoted because he emphasizes that Socrates will sooner or later get around to testing a man's life even if he starts out testing the man's thesis (*La* 187e-188c). What Laches says is that he is willing to learn from and be refuted by someone, only if the person to whom he submits himself is a good person. Laches says he will submit to Socrates because Socrates' words and deeds are in harmony. For Laches, this harmony is the only measure of the truth which a person speaks (188c-189c).

A standard of morality and truth is presupposed and depicted in the drama of the discourse; it is not legislated as a formality from outside of the discourse. Sincerity is a moral quality of character that emerges from the interactions between Socrates and the interlocutors, and it is used to gauge the interlocutor's integrity and to guide Socrates in how to proceed. The idea that a person speaks the truth only if his words are backed up by deeds goes beyond the sincerity demand. In this sense, it is a psychological feature which makes SM a normative rather than a purely formal method. Socrates says to Callicles by way of advice and reproach: 'if you catch me agreeing with you now but at a later time not doing the very things I've agreed upon (*mē tauta prattonta haper hōmologēsa*), then take me for a stupid fellow and don't bother ever afterward with lecturing me, on the ground that I'm a worthless fellow' (*Grg.* 488a9-b2, trans. Zeyl).

In refuting Meletus, Socrates illustrates not only that Meletus is easily caught in a contradiction, but that he is an irresponsible man who brings accusations against Socrates which he cannot explain and that he does not care about the youth (*Ap.* 24d, 25c, 26b, 27a). In the *Euthydemus,* the brothers are portrayed as self-defeating and ridiculous because what they say, their *logoi*, in claiming to teach virtue is not only belied by their argument that no one is ignorant or speaks falsely, it is betrayed in the way they treat Cleinias and Socrates. In the *Gorgias* (449a-461a), Socrates refutes Gorgias by deliberately driving him to an insincere belief, which Gorgias asserts out of shame because he cannot admit that he does not care whether his students know the difference between right and wrong. Socrates does this so that Gorgias will recognize the contradiction within himself that manifests, in medical terminology, as the disease of saying one thing and doing another.[23]

To dispel the idea that Socrates is always stubborn and forceful in his sincerity demand, and to show why the dialectical context is relevant, a passage from the *Theaetetus* is helpful. Socrates poses a trick question of the type that Protagoras might ask, in a debate, about relative predicates, for example in size, the taller and shorter; in number, the lesser or greater: 'can anything become greater or more without being increased?' (154c8).[24] Plato has Socrates elaborate on the problem of relative predication: we put six dice next to four and we say the six dice are *greater* but when we put six dice next to twelve we say they are *lesser*. The problem, as Plato perceives it, is a matter of language: 'that's the only way our language allows us to put it' (154c6).

Theaetetus' response is openly 'insincere' for he considers whether to answer 'no' and then 'yes' in order to avoid inconsistency in his statements. First, Socrates ironically congratulates Theaetetus for giving a fine answer, but then compares it to the response Hippolytus gives when he considers changing his mind about what he will do after having sworn to the Nurse not to divulge Phaedra's secret desire for him.[25] The point Socrates makes is that although the 'tongue is safe from refutation', the heart is not. Socrates takes the time to explain why it is important to say what one thinks, in terms of a contrast between his dialectical style which seeks to examine 'the content of [our] hearts' and the eristic or contentious style that seeks to 'put each other to the test' and 'make a contest out of it, as sophists do, and meet, with great clashing of argument on argument' (154e1-2). He goes on: '[W]hat we are really looking at is ourselves, to see what these phantoms are which lurk inside of us' (155a1-2). To finish up: Socrates and Theaetetus agree on several principles which apparently conflict with our way of expressing relative predicates, and Socrates asks Theaetetus' opinion again. Theaetetus expresses curiosity and admits *aporia* in the form of 'dizziness'. Now, Socrates utters what could be the most encouraging thing to say to someone, like Theaetetus, who has the character of a prospective student of philosophy: 'this feeling – a sense of wonder – is perfectly proper to a philosopher: philosophy has no other foundation, in fact' (155d2-4).

Sincerity and Sincere Assent

The sincerity that an interlocutor brings to the discussion determines the benefit that he can expect to receive from it. Socrates cannot force the interlocutor to be sincere. He may choose to work with what the interlocutor gives him, or he may decide to impute beliefs to the interlocutor which the interlocutor must either accept or deny. When Socrates conducts a refutation, he tests three things: the thesis, the man and the internal coherence that exists between them. I suggest that one reason why Socrates sets aside the sincerity demand, in certain cases, is that he is interested in testing all three aspects, and because he understands how the three aspects are connected, if he is unable to test one, he will test the other.[26]

Socrates is interested in the interlocutor's moral beliefs mainly because such beliefs reveal the condition of his soul. His aim is to improve the interlocutor's soul. The best way he knows to do this is to use the elenctic function to reveal contradictions in the interlocutor's belief set, and allow the interlocutor to discover for himself which belief needs to be eliminated to restore consistency. However, Socrates tries to further this process by leading the interlocutor indirectly to the view that Socrates thinks is correct. This will be the work of the protreptic function.

There is a crucial distinction to be made between 'overt' and 'covert' beliefs which is relevant to sincerity.[27] An overt belief is one that the interlocutor consciously recognizes as his own and a covert belief is one that he does not recognize he has; there are any number of reasons why he may not recognize this. Covert beliefs would include any beliefs entailed by the belief expressed of which the interlocutor is unaware. The distinction is relevant to the sincerity issue because if 'believe' is taken in an covert sense, then Socrates can target certain beliefs the interlocutor has regardless of whether he thinks he holds them or not. This extension of meaning automatically compromises the sincerity demand and deserves more attention than Vlastos gives it.

For instance, Polus has claimed in all sincerity to believe the thesis p, doing injustice is better than suffering it. Socrates tells Polus that Polus does not really believe p, and claims that he can show not only that Polus believes the opposite, *not-p*, but also that everyone else believes *not-p*. In other words, while Polus overtly believes p, he covertly believes *not-p*. Socrates is confident that he can show this because Polus will admit, as Polus is about to do at 474c7-9, that he overtly believes the premise q, doing injustice is more shameful. If Polus overtly believes q, and admits this, then Socrates is sure that he can show that Polus covertly believes *not-p* because Socrates has a way of showing that q implies *not-p*. Hence, Polus covertly believes that doing injustice is not really better than suffering injustice.

If it is legitimate for Socrates to refute the interlocutor by drawing upon beliefs that the interlocutor is not consciously committed to, either because the interlocutor does not know what his beliefs imply or because he has not considered himself well enough to recognize what he truly believes, then the sincerity demand must be qualified to reflect this type of exception. Callicles later points out that, in his view, Polus was not sincere when he agreed to q (doing injustice is more shameful than suffering it), but Polus was too ashamed to admit that he did not believe it (482e). Callicles might be right, but it could also be the case that Polus was not sharp enough to realize what he was admitting to when he agreed to Socrates' interpretation of the meaning of admirable and shameful. If Socrates can impute a belief to an interlocutor, in this extended sense, then it seems to make no difference ultimately whether or not the interlocutor is sincere. This example shows how the psychological implications of the sincerity demand alter the dialectic and affect SM.

For Socrates, there is, at least, one belief which is true regardless of what the interlocutor claims to be the case because it belongs to human nature – this is the belief that all people want what is really good. For Socrates, this is a deep psychological truth about human nature that is substantially different from the endoxical premise that all people want the apparent good, or want what they think is best. The distinction between the psychological truth which Socrates maintains and the endoxical premise that Polus argues for is illustrated in the first refutation of Polus (466b-468e). The psychological point that Socrates tries to make with Polus is not about what Polus says he sincerely believes, or the implications of what he believes, but about what the soul actually desires. This highly unusual sense of 'believe' is pursued further and explicitly addressed by Socrates in the second refutation of Polus (474b-475c).

With Polus, and Callicles, the question of sincerity is superseded because the point Socrates wants to make with them is not relevant to what they *think* they believe, whether or not it is sincere. For instance, Callicles sincerely believes that he is not someone who caters to the whims of the Athenian *dēmos*, yet Socrates will argue that Callicles' position on power and rhetoric actually commits him to this belief. The overall point Socrates labors to make is that what is actually in accordance with human nature and the desire for the good is incompatible with the kind of life and values which Polus and Callicles espouse. What supports this Socratic standpoint is what I identify as the major presupposition of the method. In the next two sections, I give a very brief account of shame and then present the psychological principle of eudaimonism which shows that the SM is founded on what Socrates believes is true about human nature.

Socratic Method and Shame

Shame is a painful and negative feeling, similar to fear, that occurs in response to being seen or caught doing, or saying, something that is wrong, or something that violates ordinary standards of decency.[28] In contrast to this type of outward-directed shame associated with the conventional view is the inner-directed shame that Socrates endorses; a third type of shame is the 'natural' shame that Callicles represents which is strongly opposed to the conventional moral shame. In Plato's dialogues, the interlocutor's sense of shame and Socrates' awareness of his own shame contribute to the aura of the dialectic that takes place between them. In the *Gorgias*, the idea is central and the contrast between the three types of shame is part of the argumentation.[29]

As a general rule, the interlocutors wish to avoid shame and they feel ashamed at being defeated in a refutation. Socrates, on the other hand, believes that they ought to be more ashamed of avoiding refutation and remaining in a state of perpetual ignorance about themselves. Socrates is portrayed as someone who does not feel shame based on what other people think. In the *Crito*, Crito appeals to Socrates' sense of shame in trying to convince him to escape from prison (46a-b), on the one hand, and, on the other hand, the personified Laws appeal to shame when they warn Socrates that he will bring shame upon himself if he breaks the law and escapes (53d-54c). The dilemma is an example of the tensions and incongruities that surround the meaning of shame in Athens in the late fifth century.

The issues raised between Socrates and Crito, or Socrates and Polus, for example, are at the heart of what is known as the '*nomos/phusis*' debate. The clash between old and new values intensified due to the political conflicts caused by the pressures of the Peloponnesian War. The traditional norms of moral behavior and the language used to express these values were challenged by a new political perspective, which used the language of self-interest. These changes were reflected in the split between *nomos*, the social/moral values of the community which regulate conduct, and *phusis*, the values of the self-interested agent who seeks to govern his conduct according to a standard set by human passions and desires. Callicles explains the antithesis quite well: by *nomos*, it is just for everyone to settle for equal shares and shameful to try to get more for oneself; by *phusis*, it is unjust to settle for equal shares since those who are stronger, by nature, deserve more, and so it is not shameful for them to do what they can to satisfy their desires (*Grg.* 482c-486d).[30]

The difference in attitudes is represented, on the one hand, by Protagoras who argues for the conventional idea that shame/respect (*aidōs*) and justice (*dikē*) are necessary for cities to exist (*Prt.* 322c-323c).[31] According to his version of the myth of Prometheus and Epimetheus, shame/respect and justice were distributed to all humans by Zeus so that they may live together in peace and prosperity, abiding by the laws. On the other hand, there are individuals like Alcibiades who pursued his political ambitions despite the harm he caused to Athens and the disrepute that he suffered for his deeds. Also, there is Antiphon, the speech-writer, politician and Sophist, who wrote a set of forensic speeches giving model arguments for both the defense and the prosecution called the *Tetralogies*. In his work, *On Truth*, he gives the argument that one need only do just deeds when witnesses are present, otherwise there is no real shame involved in doing injustice.[32]

References to what is admirable, noble or beautiful (*kalon*) and what is shameful, base or ugly (*aischron*) occur so regularly in the dialogues, it is easy to overlook the importance of these terms.[33] The dramatic action shows in subtle ways the continuous motivation on the part of the interlocutors to avoid what they perceive as shameful behavior. They often explain themselves using the emotionally charged language of *kalon* and *aischron*. For instance, Hippocrates admits he would be ashamed to be thought of as a Sophist even though he seeks to learn from Protagoras (*Prt.* 312a4-5). Lysias and Melisias are ashamed of their failures and blame their fathers for not doing more to ensure their honor and success (*La.* 179c8). Alcibiades speaks openly of the shame feelings he experiences only when he is in Socrates' presence (*Sym.* 216a-c). Phaedrus and Pausanias gives speeches on love (*erōs*) which show their extreme sensitivity to shame with regard to various homoerotic behaviors (*Sym.* 178d, 185a-b). When Socrates asks Protagoras whether he thinks that an unjust action might also be considered temperate, he says he would be 'ashamed ... to admit that, in spite of what many people say' (*Prt.* 333c1-2).

With regard to SM, commentators agree that, in some cases, Socrates makes use of the interlocutor's sense of shame at crucial moments in the refutations. But they disagree on the legitimacy of this type of appeal.[34] On first impression, it looks like Socrates merely finds the shame-based weaknesses of the interlocutor to trap him and bring him down to his knees. If this is how Socrates draws upon shame to get an interlocutor to accept a premise he might not otherwise accept, then it smacks of rhetoric and sophistry. However, this way of characterizing Socrates' use of shame as 'shame tactics' oversimplifies Socrates' motivations and flattens out the scale of values that shame represents.

As I mentioned earlier, there are different kinds of shame and, given Socrates' commitment to the value of self-knowledge, the chances are that Socrates pries into the interlocutor's psychological states to raise his awareness of his moral commitments. Self-based, inner-directed shame is constructive; it forces an awareness of one's relation to one's own moral standards and ideals. If the standards are derived from what other people think and this alone, then the interlocutor will be made to see that this is the source of shame. However, Socrates does think that there are legitimate shame feelings, not just the other-directed, conventionally based shame. So his approach is multi-leveled. Though I cannot pursue the issue in any further depth, the interlocutor's relationship to shame is one of the keys to moral improvement through self-knowledge. Socrates wants the interlocutor to persuade himself, and if he can use the interlocutor's shame to facilitate this, he will not hesitate to do so. It is up to the interlocutor to go further, however. If the interlocutor's sensitivity to shame is a sore spot, and the drama of the dialogue indicates that this is a barrier to self-awareness, then one would do well to follow where this leads.

The Psychological Principle of Eudaimonism

The general principle of eudaimonism is a normative, teleological principle which holds that all actions are done for the sake of the final good which is happiness (*Grg.* 467d-468e; cf. 499e, 509e; *La.* 185a-186c; *Ly.* 219c-220b). Psychological eudaimonism is a claim about human nature which holds that human beings desire the good, or what is conducive to their final good, or happiness. Psychological eudaimonism can also be expressed by the Socratic paradox that no one does evil knowing that it is evil. In the *Meno*, for instance, when Meno proposes the definition that virtue is the desire and ability to obtain good things (77b-c), Socrates asks Meno, 'Do not all men ... desire the good?' (*tōn agathōn epithumein*). When Meno replies that he thinks some men desire evil knowing that it is evil, Socrates gets Meno to admit that no one wants (*bouletai*) to be miserable, and then asks, '... for what is being miserable but desiring evil and obtaining it?' (78a9). Meno concedes, 'It seems that what you say is true, Socrates, and that nobody desires evil' (*oudeis boulesthai ta kaka*). The refutation rests on the Socratic premise that the desire for good 'belongs to our common nature' (78b6-7).

   In the *Apology* (25e-26a), Socrates argues that he does not intentionally corrupt his associates because to do so would mean that he wanted to harm himself. He implies that no one would want this. Socrates puts the point in extreme terms, when he asks Meletus if Meletus thinks that he is in '... such a depth of ignorance that I do not even know this, that if I make anyone [*sic*] of my associates bad I am in danger of getting some harm from him, so that I do this great evil voluntarily, as you say? I don't believe this, Meletus, nor do I think anyone else in the world does ...' (25e3-8). In the *Protagoras*, the premise that no one knowingly goes towards evil is said to be true because 'it is not in human nature, apparently, to do so' (358d1-2; cf. 358e10, 345d-e). This premise, couched in the hedonistic terms that no one would go after what he knew to be painful, secures the refutation of Protagoras, and supports the Socratic view that all of the virtues are one and the same thing, knowledge. In the *Euthydemus* (278e4-5), psychological eudaimonism is treated as obvious, 'Do all we human beings wish to prosper? . . . for I suppose it is stupid merely to ask such things, since every man must wish to prosper' (*boulometha eu prattein*).[35]

The truth of the claim that all humans desire the good is fundamental to the philosophical progress of the SM. Socrates always supposes that despite whatever the interlocutor may think is happening to him as a result of his refutation, the refutation is a good thing. If refutation is a good thing, then the interlocutor's soul really desires it, that is, in the Socratic sense, where 'desire' indicates a 'lack of something which belongs to that thing by nature'.[36] In the Socratic view, there is a tacit assumption always operating that what is good for the interlocutor is what is good for his soul.[37] Evidence for this assumption is explicit in some dialogues, and sometimes the assumption accompanies the principle of psychological eudaimonism. For instance, in the *Gorgias*, after getting Polus to agree that '. . . the one paying what is due has good things being done to him', and is 'being benefited', Socrates asks, 'Is his benefit the one I take it to be? Does his soul undergo improvement if he is justly disciplined?' Polus says that it is likely (477a-b).

In my view, the Socratic method is justifiably the proper method for educating the soul, given the Socratic psychological principle that it is in the nature of the soul to desire the good and it operates in conjunction with the Socratic moral belief that virtue is always good, or beneficial, to the soul. The pattern of reasoning constitutes a 'protreptic argument' which I will discuss in detail in the next chapter. In general, it runs like this. If the only thing that is truly good is the knowledge of how to use subordinate goods, then this knowledge is the proper object of human desire. Human well-being, or happiness, depends on the knowledge of how to benefit the soul. The knowledge of how to use subordinate goods to benefit or care for the soul is the knowledge that Socrates believes everyone desires, and philosophers consciously seek. The subordinate goods are the means that are good or bad only in accordance with how they are used (cf. *Eud.* 278e-282d; *Meno* 87e-89a). Knowledge of proper use of the subordinate goods is knowledge that is guided by a moral purpose to improve oneself and others.[38]

This knowledge is both prudential and moral. It is prudential because having this kind of knowledge is in the interest of the soul, and the soul is the moral source of one's well-being. The strong conceptual connection that exists between prudential and moral domains which Socrates plays upon has to do with motivation and desire. In Socrates' view, 'desire for the good' is not the same as the 'desire for the apparent good', defined as a matter of what an individual agent *thinks* he wants. Like Polus, an agent may think he wants power and pleasure, or he may think that he does not want to be refuted. He is wrong because he does not know the nature of his soul and that the true object of his soul's desire is the goodness which is wisdom.

Conclusion: A Constructive Approach

The central disagreement I have with Vlastos' account is his attempt to force the SM into a deductive framework, and to discuss the shortcomings of the method as a failure to meet a demonstrative criterion of truth which is inappropriate for the method. Vlastos also relies on this framework in his claim that the *elenchos* is the sole support for Socrates' substantive views. What underlies this claim is that if Socrates is unable to establish the truth of his doctrine demonstratively, then Socrates is some kind of dogmatist who puts forth doctrine without proper justification. Except for the *Gorgias*, Socrates rarely presents his views in a dogmatic way, and given the context and characters of the *Gorgias*, his forceful approach is warranted. On this interpretation, if Socrates does not derive his views from argumentation similar to that given in the 'early' dialogues, there is no other way he could establish them as true.

To explain how Socrates is none the less justified in holding the premises true and the conclusions of his arguments established, Vlastos is driven, in a roundabout way, to an inductive explanation, and to the concept of elenctic knowledge. In this way, Vlastos finds that demonstrative certainty cannot be the kind of truth which Socrates aims at in his philosophical activity. However, demonstrative certainty could have been eliminated as a possible criterion of truth in the method simply by reference to what Socrates says in the *Apology* about the value of human wisdom in comparison to the divine (20d-e, 23a-c). Once complete and certain knowledge is ruled out and assigned to the gods, dialectical argument and irrefutability seem to be the best test a human being can have for truth. This second-best criterion of truth provides the framework for understanding why mutual agreement and consistency play such an important role in the *elenchos*.

Although it is not plausible to hold that individual elenctic arguments are the direct source for the truth of Socrates' moral beliefs, it might be plausible to give an inductive explanation of how Socrates justifies the confidence he has in his beliefs.[39] On this line of reasoning, Socrates validates his views by the experience of examining and defending them in continuous dialectical arguments with various interlocutors. This experience shows him that no one so far has succeeded in refuting his moral position, and this is a fair indication that Socrates maintains a consistent set of beliefs. Socrates is portrayed as debating with those who are considered the wisest of his time, and his success bolsters his confidence, yet he can never be certain that he has the truth, so he must always continue to examine others and himself. This explanation only goes so far because irrefutability in dialectical argument depends upon personal and psychological factors, and not merely upon the logic of the arguments.

Regardless of how many times the arguments are put to the test, if Socrates' arguments depend on the use of ambiguity, reinterpreted regulative endoxical premises and tacit assumptions, and if he appeals to the interlocutor's shame to weaken the interlocutor's position, then Socrates' arguments are not valid. This means that the irrefutability that is achieved through the method has a qualified meaning, and cannot be used directly to judge the soundness of Socrates' moral position. So although my interpretation of the SM is compatible with the inductive explanation of Socrates' confidence in his views, the inductive explanation loses its logical force as a way of justifying Socrates' moral beliefs.[40]

In my interpretation, Socratic moral principles are made clear in a number of ways, though the exact justification for the truth of these principles is left unexplained, for the most part.[41] Nevertheless, a Socratic moral position can be reconstructed from a clarification of the functions and goal of the method, from the tacit assumptions Socrates makes throughout the dialogues, from the direction the arguments take once he begins to lead, from the reinterpreted regulative endoxical premises which he uses and from those occasions when he simply expresses his view. Socrates' dialectical conduct, including his irony, is another source for understanding his values. Once it is recognized that Socrates' substantive views must be obtained through sources other than the conclusions of individual elenctic arguments, an abundance of textual material emerges for reconstructing a Socratic moral position.

I propose a constructive approach which addresses the interpretive problem of how to understand Socrates' moral position by attending carefully to Socrates' dialectical argumentation and Plato's dramatic art which shows us how Socrates argues indirectly for his views. In arguing for this approach, I am not so much concerned with extracting Socratic doctrine from the texts or formulating a Socratic ethics. Rather, I wish to make a strong case about the coherence between Socratic method and Socratic moral views; in other words, there is a reciprocal relation between what he does and what he says and believes. My interpretation relies upon a very strong assumption about Socratic integrity.

I also rely upon my intuitive sense of Plato as a consummate artist. My perspective, from reading Plato's dialogues, is that by dramatizing SM with extraordinary subtlety and intensity, Plato shows an overriding concern to present Socrates as a paradigm of someone who is morally and psychologically consistent. It is not just Plato's artistic talents which I credit for this but his philosophical acuity and psychological insight into the meaning of Socratic integrity and the model that this will provide for future philosophers. In response to the integrity that he must have perceived in the historical Socrates, Plato is inspired to fashion the drama of his dialogues in a way that will match the philosophical ideas which he wishes to convey.

As I have outlined in this chapter, the approach is to identify the aim and the functions of the method, its principal presupposition, and the strategies needed to make it work. I take the positive results of SM, and their connection to the Socratic moral position, in the way that Socrates appears to take them. The positive results are connected to what he believes to be the moral improvement of the interlocutor because this is his primary objective. I think that it is within the context of this objective that the justification of Socrates' method and moral position can be found rather than through an account that relies upon a direct deductive or inductive explanation of the elenctic arguments.

My approach is constructive because I think it is possible to understand what Socrates' moral position is by means of the elenctic-protreptic arguments in conjunction with the dramatic elements which Plato offers to his readers. No straightforward deductive or inductive explanation is adequate without recognizing the dialectical strategies at work which attenuate the logical force of the arguments. Keeping this qualification in mind, I believe that his moral position can be determined by giving the elenctic arguments a protreptic reading. To give an elenctic argument a protreptic reading requires (1) offering a revised Socratic interpretation of one or more of the regulative endoxical premises, (2) giving the ambiguous terms in the regulative endoxical premises a precise Socratic meaning, and (3) making several of Socrates' assumptions explicit. This is how I believe an interpreter can discover the truths which underlie the Socratic moral position, and this process has to do mainly with the protreptic function of the SM.

My constructive approach is new because it gives proper attention to the moral and psychological values which surround Socrates' construction of the arguments, and accounts for his actual dialectical behavior. In the next chapter, I develop my constructive approach by explaining the protreptic function of the method. I have yet to provide an explanation for the fourth claim (iv) that Socrates makes use of regulative *endoxa*, as a dialectical strategy. I will devote the next chapter to an explanation and defense of the fifth claim (v) that Socrates makes use of verbal ambiguity in his reinterpretation of certain regulative endoxical premises.

I have brought together a number of features which show that the SM is inextricably bound to, and clearly illustrative of, Socratic beliefs on both the moral and psychological levels. In order to understand the SM, it is important to understand how the method makes use of Socrates' moral position. I will continue to make it clear how the Socratic moral position is related to the method in my discussion of the protreptic function in the next chapter. I have not tried to justify the method in this chapter or show that the method succeeds in achieving its aim. I have presented an interpretation which puts the SM into a different framework for understanding how it can be justified and whether it does succeed.

Chapter 2

The Protreptic Function

Introduction

In the first chapter, I have offered an interpretation of SM which makes it a normative method with moral and psychological content and an informal structure. The moral content given by Socrates' aim is to improve himself and others through self-knowledge. There is a set of dialectical functions which serve the aim. The interpretation is predominantly psychological due to the existential and personal features of *aporia*, sincerity and shame as well as Socrates' reliance on the principle of psychological eudaimonism that all humans desire the good (hereinafter referred to as the 'eudaimonist principle'). This principle has great significance in my account of SM since it presupposes a view of human nature and motivation; it raises semantic questions about the meanings of the terms 'good', 'desire' and the concept of *erōs*. Further, the principle includes Socrates' tacit assumptions about the soul: the soul is rational, it is the locus of desire, and the highest source of value.

In this chapter, I show that SM is revisionist and involves a persuasive strategy which makes use of three regulative endoxical premises and ambiguity. This type of strategy enables Socrates to carry out the functions of refuting and persuading the interlocutor at the same time. The plan of the chapter is to clarify the nature of this strategy by examining the themes, discourse and lines of argument related to Socratic protreptic. By 'Socratic protreptic', I mean all of the dialectical activities Socrates brings to bear to motivate his interlocutors to reorientate their values, pursue wisdom/virtue and live the philosophical life.

The chapter begins by developing more fully two modes of discourse and their function in argumentation with an emphasis on the protreptic function. I discuss the concept of *endoxon* (pl. *endoxa*) – common or reputable opinion – and show its relevance to SM as a method of persuasion. The interlocutors are classified into four major groups as a way of showing which type of character is most receptive to Socratic protreptic and likely to benefit from it. Then, I examine the dialogues to illustrate the themes of Socratic protreptic and discuss several passages which best exemplify the protreptic lines of argument. Finally, I single out three endoxical premises which Socrates uses in his elenctic arguments and suggest how these endoxical premises are transformed into protreptic premises.

The Elenctic and Protreptic Functions

The Elenctic Function

It is part of my project to explain how the elenctic and protreptic aspects of the method coexist and function in cooperation with each other in Socrates' practice of philosophy. I think that this cooperative dialectical activity is what makes SM a unique and very complicated philosophical method. To begin this section, I review briefly the logical structure of the Socratic *elenchos*, which I have designated the 'elenctic function' of SM. In elenctic argumentation, Socrates usually refutes the interlocutor's thesis p by showing that p is inconsistent with other premises, q, r, s, the truth of which the interlocutor accepts and is unlikely to give up. On this basis, Socrates is able to conclude *not-p*. I maintain that, in most cases, the interlocutor's thesis is not genuinely refuted because the argument Socrates constructs is typically invalid due to his use of ambiguity of the key terms which occur primarily in the agreed-upon premises.

As I interpret SM, the interlocutor often accepts a premise q, r or s, because it is endoxical and he takes the meaning of the terms conventionally as they would be used in everyday discourse. In the process of the argumentation, the meaning of the premise changes because a Socratic sense is given to the terms. The premise becomes ambiguous and is subject to two very different interpretations. One interpretation represents the interlocutor's belief and another interpretation represents Socrates' belief, in which case it will be interpreted morally. There are three endoxical premises (to be introduced shortly) which occur with sufficient regularity in the elenctic arguments to warrant a special dialectical status. These same endoxical premises are given a Socratic interpretation and will be alternatively construed and designated as protreptic premises. 'Protreptic premises' are those which correspond to premises which are *prima facie* endoxical but when turned around in meaning come to represent Socrates' moral position.[1] Such premises are called 'protreptic' because they are imbued with a Socratic meaning and projected ideally on to the interlocutor as what he would believe if he knew himself better.

Clearly, there is more to the elenctic function than its logical structure. Moreover, the refutations Socrates conducts do not occur as isolated activities. The elenctic function has an immediate aim, *aporia*, which must be understood in light of the larger aim of SM. It also involves a characteristic mode of discourse and a number of identifiably distinct stages. First, Socrates asks questions and formulates an interpretation of the interlocutor's intended meaning which gives philosophical content to a proposed thesis. Second, the thesis is attributed to the interlocutor on the basis of his responses. Third, he secures the interlocutor's agreement to a set of premises, one or more of which are endoxical, i.e. those which reflect popular opinion or derive from a commonly accepted authority. Fourth, using the interlocutor's agreement to the premises, Socrates constructs an elenctic argument which results in a conclusion that contradicts the original thesis. Fifth, the interlocutor experiences some degree of *aporia*. Once this takes place, there is a shift in the inter-personal dynamics of the conversation and the dialogue takes a positive direction.

What happens next depends on the structure of the dialogue. If the dialogue has a single interlocutor, then Socrates' role in leading the discussion becomes more explicit and he may openly contribute his own views. There is a general feeling that progress is being made towards solving the problem which caused the *aporia* of the dialogue. If there is a second or third interlocutor, the drama intensifies and the dialogue advances to a more complex level of questioning. In either case, near the end of the dialogue, an obstacle is created which prevents closure, and success is, in my view, deliberately subverted, but only after some strong suggestions have been implanted as to how to conceptualize the problem. The drama ends, perhaps, with Socrates' ironic humor or hortatory remarks about continuing the investigation. Examples of the first pattern occur in the *Euthyphro* (11e), *Meno* (81a), and when Crito agrees to set the majority view aside (*Cr.* 48b-49b). Examples of the second are when Critias takes over for Charmides (162c), and with Critias himself, a step is advanced when Socrates grants the point that knowledge of knowledge may be possible (*Chrm.* 169d), and moves on to question whether it is beneficial. Nicias takes over from Laches; Polemarchus becomes the heir to the argument from Cephalus.[2] Once Polemarchus is refuted, Thrasymachus takes over the discussion. A similar type of dialectical movement occurs in three stages with Gorgias, Polus and Callicles. In conjunction with the elenctic mode of discourse, there is another mode of discourse that is required because Socrates must interpret the interlocutor's meaning as he constructs the argument. This is how the protreptic function operates.

The Protreptic Function

The protreptic function is a persuasive dialectical activity in the sense that Socratic terminology and beliefs play an active role in how Socrates constructs the arguments. Socrates does not construct arguments simply to refute the interlocutor or to test the truth of the thesis; he attempts to lead the interlocutor to a Socratic moral position. That is to say, he tries to influence the content of the interlocutor's beliefs. As I hope to show, he does not do this by improperly 'exploiting' the ambiguity of evaluative language for fun and games; rather, he puts the ambiguity to constructive use. He utilizes the ambiguity in language, in a conscientious way, to revise and expand upon the ordinary meaning of evaluative terms, as these terms are accepted by the interlocutors in their current usage. In effect, Socrates re-conceptualizes the meaning of key terms and gives them an expanded, philosophical meaning while he constructs an elenctic argument or a series of elenctic arguments.

There are two ways in which Socratic protreptic operates, directly and indirectly. Socrates sometimes encourages the interlocutor directly through simple exhortation. In some dialogues when Socrates meets the interlocutor, he must first encourage the interlocutor to begin the inquiry, for instance with Charmides and, from the dramatic perspective, Crito who least of all has time to consider reasons why Socrates ought to remain in prison. In other cases, he has to urge the interlocutor to continue with him, despite setbacks, and carry on the inquiry to the end. This kind of coaxing occurs at crucial stages in the conversation.

For instance, at a critical moment when Polus must answer and admit that he has been refuted, Socrates says, 'but submit yourself nobly (*gennaiōs*) to the argument, as to a doctor, and reply yes or no to my question' (*Grg.* 475d9-10). After Meno has stifled the inquiry by raising his paradox of learning (80d-e), Socrates speaks to him about 'the duty of inquiring after what we do not know', saying that this 'will make us better and braver and less helpless' (*Meno* 86b-c; cf. 81d-e). When Critias complains that Socrates is simply trying to refute him (*Chrm.* 166c3-8), Socrates defends his motivation and says that his purpose is to examine the argument and discover the truth about the matter at hand, for the 'common good' of everyone involved (166c9-d7). Critias acknowledges Socrates' point; Socrates says, 'Then take heart . . . and answer the question put to you . . . without caring whether it is Critias or Socrates who is being refuted: give the argument itself your attention and observe what will become of it under the test of refutation' (166d9-e3). In the *Laches*, a dialogue about courage, Socrates says to Laches, 'let us be steadfast and enduring in our inquiry' (194a1-3). Socrates commends Glaucon for his spirit in sticking with the inquiry (*Rep.* I 357a). In the *Cratylus*, Socrates exhorts himself not to 'play the coward' (411a-b), and at the end of a long debate he advises Cratylus, who is too willing to accept a Heraclitean theory of names, 'to consider courageously and thoroughly and not accept anything carelessly' (440d4-7).[3]

To carry on with the examples a bit further. Socrates gives Theodorus, who retreats from taking active part in the dialectic, a suitable admonitory exhortation:

> Do not go on imagining that it is my business to be straining every nerve to defend your dear friend while you do nothing. Come now, my very good Theodorus, come a little way with me ... try a fall with me and we shall both be the better (168e-169c, cf. 177b-c, trans. Levett).

At the dramatic level, the direct exhortations are often appropriate to the attributes of the characters with whom Socrates interacts. At the textual level, the exhortations are urgent calls to the mind, or the whole self which is the soul, to engage critically in the practice of philosophy. At both levels, the direct protreptic is needed for there is intellectual work involved. The dialectic demands that one desires to learn and that one has the mental tenacity to stick with the arguments in their worse moments. Plato dramatizes the exasperation of the interlocutors and probably expects that his readers will feel the same.

The forms of persuasion in the dialogues go far beyond the regular calls to apply one's mind to the problem at hand. Plato's Socrates has another, more intractable means to grab the attention of the intellect of those who try to follow the argumentation and manage, perhaps, to find some problems with the reasoning. This type of engagement is like working out a puzzle or riddle; it is intellectually challenging, morally beneficial, and psychologically appealing to the minds of those listeners and readers who find constructive ideas in the dialectical activity of the dialogues. The by-product of this mental engagement is not neutral; it is infiltrated with Socrates' moral position and is 'indirectly' protreptic. This indirect protreptic activity is my concern for the rest of this discussion and throughout the book.

The indirect protreptic approach has to do with the persuasion that is contained in the arguments that take place between Socrates and the interlocutor. The arguments which Socrates uses are meant to persuade the interlocutor to change his moral views by means of a discovery of what is implicit in the premises that he has already agreed to in the argument. As Socrates leads the inquiry, he tries to move the interlocutor and the whole framework of the discussion towards the consideration of a Socratic position. This movement from a conventional moral standpoint to a Socratic standpoint is a constant work-in-progress in the dialectic.

The protreptic function is indirect because it is governed by the question-and-answer format and Socrates must work from within the interlocutor's belief system to get his expressed agreement to the premises. The immediate aim of the protreptic function is to get the interlocutors to realize how the revised concepts and reconsidered premises can fit into their belief systems. Socrates does this by suggesting a new evaluative context for making moral judgments and guiding conduct; he promotes the soul as the proper framework. I construe the SM as a revisionist method because it attempts to change the meaning of the endoxical beliefs the interlocutor already has by conceptual reorientation. This is an interpretive activity and it explains the significance of Socrates' use of ambiguity, his use of regulative *endoxa* and his attempt to find common ground on which to base his arguments, because in order to change the way the interlocutors perceive their moral experience, Socrates must draw upon that experience at its most fundamental level.

The protreptic function motivates Socrates' effort to find premises that the interlocutor agrees to, which will also turn out be true on a Socratic interpretation. For this reason, I think the Socratic use of ambiguity and other fallacies has a legitimate role to play in SM. The protreptic discourse involves not only the arguments that Socrates constructs to persuade the interlocutor, but rhetorical techniques of persuasion as well. Such rhetorical techniques are his direct exhortations, verbal irony, insincere praise and exaggerated self-criticism, the appeal to the interlocutor's sense of shame, the strategic maneuvers in directing the discourse and setting up the arguments, and the power of his personal character.

Examples from the Texts

Within the dramatic context of the dialogues, Plato shows the reader what it is that Socrates does and the effects he has on his interlocutors. From time to time, Socrates describes his methodology and comments on his motives for engaging in dialectic. Although Socrates is ironic and indirect about his motives, there are aspects of his methodology which can be gathered from his repeated remarks to others about the nature of his practice and his immediate aims. Socrates clearly refers to all three functions in the dialogues. In my view, Plato expects the reader to see how these functions exist side by side, and I fervently believe that he expects the reader to recognize that there are problems with the smooth operation of these functions. I mention only a few examples here, but there will be ample opportunity for me to present other cases and elaborate on the difficulties that are raised.

The elenctic and epistemic functions, for example, are mentioned in the *Protagoras*. After the Simonides' poem episode, Socrates rejects the idea that the dialectical partners should invest their time and energy in interpreting the poets. So, he says, 'It is the truth, and our minds, that we should be testing' (348a4-5). Socrates openly claims that his motive for asking questions and constructing arguments is to seek truth. The argument (*logos*) is sometimes depersonalized, 'The inquiry remains quite incapable of discovering the truth' (*Chrm.* 175d1-2; cf. 165b8–9, 166c8-e2), and sometimes personified, '[O]ur discussion, in its present result, seems to me as though it accused and mocked us like some human person' (*Prt.* 361a-b).

References to learning and teaching are sometimes made ironically, as when Socrates tells Euthyphro, 'the best thing I can do is to become your pupil, and challenge Meletus before the trial comes on' (*Eu.* 5a3-5). Heavy-handed irony is used with regard to the education offered by the Sophists in the *Euthydemus* (272b1-2, d1-3; 297b7, d6-7). Socrates gladly assures Hippias about his good intentions, 'I am not ashamed to learn, and I ask and inquire, and am very grateful to those who answer me ... and when I learn a thing I never deny my teacher, or pretend that the lesson is a discovery of my own' (*HMin.* 372c1-8; cf. 369e1). Socrates asks Glaucon, with reference to Thrasymachus, 'Do you wish us then to try to persuade him, supposing we can find a way, that what he says is not true?' (*Rep.* I 348a3–4). Laches is disgruntled and claims that Nicias is covering up his own perplexity and talking nonsense. Socrates responds that it is best to ask Nicias to explain what he means, 'and if we find that he means something, we will agree with him; if not, we will instruct him' (*La.* 196c3-4).

Numerous references to the activity of persuasion occur in the *Apology*, *Crito*, *Euthydemus* and *Gorgias* due to their dramatic contexts. In his defense speech, Socrates tells the Athenian jury that he will not stop engaging in his investigations and in philosophy, nor will he 'stop exhorting you and pointing out the truth to any one of you whom I may meet' (*Ap.* 29d5-6). He admonishes them because they do not care enough for their souls and are preoccupied with money and honor. He says that they ought to be ashamed for not caring about 'wisdom and truth' and the best possible state of their souls (29e1–2). Socrates says:

> and if any of you argues the point and says he does care, I shall not let him go at once, nor shall I go away, but will question and examine and cross-examine him; and if I find that he does not possess virtue but says he does,

I shall rebuke him for scorning the things of most importance and caring more for what is of less worth (*Ap.* 29e3-30a1).

Socrates is engaging in what he considers to be 'care of the soul' (*epimeleia tēs psuchēs*)[4] or 'therapy for the soul' (*therapeuesthai de tēn psuchēn*).[5] S. R. Slings calls Socrates' emphasis on care of the soul 'the central concept of Socratic exhortation'. He points out that Socratic protreptic involves an 'accusatory' aspect which can be seen in the above passage and in what follows.[6]

Given the chance to propose a counter-penalty rather than be put to death, Socrates continues with his protreptic style of speech:

And what do I deserve to suffer or to pay, because in my life I did not keep quiet, but neglecting what most men (*hoi polloi*) care for – money making and property, and offices and plots and parties that come up in the state – and thinking that I was really too honorable to engage in those activities and live, refrained from those things by which I should have been no use (*mēdan ophelos einai*) to you or myself and devoted myself to conferring (*euergetein*) upon each citizen individually what I regard as the greatest benefit (*tēn megistēn euergesian*)? For I tried to persuade (*pethein*) each of you to care for himself and his own perfection in goodness (*beltistos*) and wisdom (*phronimōtatos*) rather than for any of his belongings and for the state itself rather than for its interests . . . (*Ap.* 36b4-c8).

It is clear that SM has a protreptic function that is grounded in his concern for the condition of the interlocutor's soul. Socrates attempts to persuade the interlocutor that he ought to care for his soul by pursuing virtue and loving wisdom.

Other examples with regard to persuasion are as follows. Socrates says to Protagoras, 'Come then, and join me in the endeavor to persuade the world and explain what is this experience of theirs, which they call "being overcome by pleasure"' (*Prt.* 352e9-10). Socrates tells Lysimachus that he will first listen to what Laches and Nicias have to say, 'and then, if I have anything else to suggest as against their remarks, I might try to explain it and persuade you (*didaskein kai peithein*) and them to take my view' (*La.* 181d8-9). In the *Apology*, Socrates uses the same locution (*didaskein kai peithein*) when he says that rather than supplicate the judge, one ought 'to inform and convince him' (35c2).

The Use of *Endoxa*

The term '*endoxa*' refers to the commonly accepted or reputable opinions of the times. This is the sense that Aristotle gives to the term, in the *Topics*, where he defines endoxical beliefs as 'those accepted by everyone or by the majority or by the wise' (100b21-22).[7] For most Athenians, endoxical beliefs are treated as knowledge, the truths of which are grounded in tradition and convention which are influenced by the teachings of the poets, prophets, rhetors, military and political leaders.[8] In the dialectical context, *endoxa* provide the crucial starting points which Socrates relies upon to establish a common ground of agreement. Endoxical premises are treated as assumptions which are *prima facie* true; typically they need no further justification though at times they may be given additional empirical support.[9] In this section, I argue for the thesis that the method not only uses endoxical premises, but it depends quite heavily on them as a dialectical strategy. Further, I suggest that Socrates' combined use of regulative *endoxa* and ambiguity shows how he is able to argue for his own moral position.

In an effort to clarify the topic, there is an important distinction between two applications of the concept of *endoxa* that must be made. The distinction is one which pertains to the role of endoxical beliefs in moral inquiry, for example what governs and guides Socrates in his questioning; and that which pertains to the object of the inquiry, for example what, in fact, constitutes the interlocutor's moral values and conduct. In accordance with the distinction, *endoxa* are understood as either 'regulative' or 'substantive'.[10] Regulative *endoxa* are used to guide an inquiry because they are reasonable to accept and relatively uncontroversial. Substantive *endoxa* are the conventional moral opinions or norms that guide conduct.

Regulative endoxical premises play an instrumental role in dialectical inquiry and argument. They are often, though not always, taken for granted and for the most part, Socrates has no problem getting assent. The regulative use of endoxical beliefs as premises in an argument must be kept distinct from the substantive *endoxa* which are the popular conceptions of virtue, the moral attitudes and life-guiding goals which Socrates' interlocutors espouse. In making this distinction I do not mean that the regulative *endoxa* are insubstantial or empty of content, but only that they are the constant or routine beliefs that Socrates relies upon in his questioning. The use of regulative endoxical premises in SM does not commit Socrates to accepting any substantive endoxical belief as true.

On the contrary, Socrates wishes to refute the substantive endoxical belief that the interlocutor initially proposes, for example the original thesis p, which is technically called the 'refutand'. A regulative endoxical premise is either explicitly introduced to get the interlocutor's consent or it is tacitly accepted among other things being agreed upon, for example these are the premises q, r, s. The set of premises will then be used to overthrow the refutand. The compelling nature of the whole reasoning process is due to the regulative endoxical beliefs. They are simple, accessible and difficult to deny, hence Socrates is able to get swift, unreflective agreement to the premises he needs to overthrow the original thesis.

There are places in the texts where Socrates explicitly appeals to the unanimity of a belief. At *Ion* 532c-d, 'It's clear to everyone that you are unable to speak about Homer with art and knowledge. For if you could, you'd be able to speak about all the other poets too', and 'Anybody can tell what I meant in saying it's the same inquiry when one understands an art as a whole' (532e, trans. Allen). Socrates questions Euthyphro about his definition of piety as the 'art of barter between gods and men'; Socrates exclaims, 'For everybody knows what they give, since we have nothing good which they do not give. But what advantage do they derive from what they get from us?' (14e5-15a5). In his discussion with Diotima, Socrates insists that 'everybody in the world' agrees that Erōs is a 'great god' (*Sym.* 202b6-10). The belief that 'we all wish to be happy and have good things' is said to need no further justification (*Sym.* 205a1-5; *Eud.* 278e-279a).

Socrates frequently depends upon the ordinariness and common sense of the premises, and, of course, the poets. In defending himself against Meletus, Socrates asks whether it is true that the few rather than the many are skilled with horses. He makes the reply himself: 'Certainly it is, whether you or Anytus deny it or agree' (*Ap.* 28b7-8). When Charmides defines the virtue of temperance (*sōphrosunē*) as 'quietness', Socrates points out that some acts which are fine or admirable are carried out swiftly (159b-160d). Charmides next defines *sōphrosunē* as 'shame' (*aidōs*), and Socrates appeals to Homer to show that *aidōs* is not always a good thing (160e-161b). There are many endoxical beliefs and subjects to choose from to regulate the inquiry, such as friendship (*philia*). Socrates is careful in his selection. In the *Lysis*, 'like is friend to like', according to Homer (213d-215c), and 'unlike is friend to unlike', according to Hesiod (215c-216b). Again, with Callicles, Socrates says, 'It seems to me that the closest possible friendship between man and man is that mentioned by the sages of old time as 'like to like' (*Grg.* 510b5-6).

Other premises are taken to be true because they are logically compelling, such as 'each single opposite has but one opposite, not many' (*Prt.* 332c10), and 'doing well and faring badly are opposite states' (*Grg.* 495e2-3).[11] Further, Socrates says to Protagoras, who supposedly speaks for the many, that 'you know well enough for yourselves that the erring act committed without knowledge is done through ignorance' (357d10-e2). Some premises are psychologically compelling as well: *Socrates*: 'What I mean is, will a man avoid being wronged by merely wishing not to be wronged, or will he avoid it by providing himself with power to avert it?' *Callicles*: 'The answer to that is obvious: by means of power' (509d5).

The use of regulative *endoxa* as a dialectical strategy is distinct from the sincerity demand that is attributed to SM. The use of regulative *endoxa* does not interfere with sincerity, for as long as the interlocutor genuinely accepts a belief, endoxical or otherwise, as his own, the sincerity demand is satisfied. However, once the interlocutor accepts an endoxical premise as his own, the premise though ascribed to him does not cease to be endoxical in origin.[12] The sincerity demand is supposed to guarantee that the interlocutor's stated belief is his own, but by itself, the demand does not determine the exact source of the truth for the interlocutor. It is Socrates' use of regulative *endoxa* that is effective in helping him to determine the rational basis for the interlocutor's belief. My understanding of what it means for the interlocutor to accept a premise as his own is that the interlocutor becomes responsible for defending the truth of that premise, independently of the source of his belief with regard to that premise which he may or may not wish to acknowledge. Some interlocutors try to avoid making the belief their own and taking responsibility for it; they would rather assume that the substantive endoxical status of the belief will suffice as an explanation for why the thesis is true.

As the examples show, when Socrates examines the interlocutors, they usually attempt to state their initial thesis by citing a maxim or formula taken from a source of authority, the poets, the Sophists, the majority view or even a Socratic view. Polemarchus cites Simonides, Meno cites Gorgias, Hippias cites Homer, Nicias implicitly relies on what he heard from Socrates. Crito and Polus cite the many. An interesting case is that of Protagoras who refuses to align himself with the views of the many but Socrates pushes the connection anyway because Protagoras has given a great speech on behalf of their beliefs. Charmides appeals to Critias' opinion that temperance (*sōphrosunē*) is 'doing one's own' but fails to understand its meaning. Critias cites Hesiod to defend his position. In these cases (except for Protagoras' view as noted), Socrates separates the interlocutor's stated belief from the endoxical source of that belief, and he makes sure that the belief is one that the interlocutor endorses. This is the purpose of the sincerity demand. Once the interlocutor is committed to the belief, the sincerity demand is satisfied, but the endoxical source of that belief remains. The sincerity demand is extremely useful because Socrates can proceed to examine both the interlocutor's belief and the substantive *endoxa*, at the same time. Socrates' reliance upon sincerity and *endoxa* in just this way forms part of his persuasive strategy.

Regulative endoxical beliefs are valuable to SM because they help Socrates to get the interlocutor's agreement. As agreed-upon premises, they provide Socrates with a dialectical tool for reinterpreting the meaning of the central concepts in the premises and he can use them to refute and

persuade the interlocutor. Once a regulative endoxical premise is introduced in a refutation and accepted, Socrates uses ambiguity to reinterpret
its meaning, and in this way, the regulative premise is transformed and gains
substantive moral import. The combined use of regulative *endoxa* and verbal
ambiguity is tricky and complex; none the less, I believe that this strategy is
fundamentally a distinctive feature of SM.

In my discussion of *endoxa*, I am primarily concerned with Socrates' use of
regulative *endoxa* as one or more of the agreed-upon premises and I shall
limit my discussion to three such premises which I believe form an important set for SM. The specific premises, in their most general formulations,
are: 'all humans desire the good' (D); 'virtue is beneficial' (B); and 'virtue
is like a *technē*' (T).

To conclude this section, I would like to make clear what I am calling the
protreptic function. It is an indirect form of persuasion by which Socrates
uses the ambiguity of evaluative language to reinterpret the regulative
endoxical premises. It is a vital part of SM that Socrates put forward a protreptic argument which represents his moral position. Such arguments can
be reconstructed within a given elenctic argument or series of arguments.
Interpreting Socrates' protreptic activity is not only a matter of analysing
the arguments but attending carefully to the internal frame of the dialogue, e.g. the dramatic signals and tensions, the psychological attributes of
the characters, and allowances for Socrates' ironic humor. Along with the
dialectical nuances and dramatic details which belong to the internal
frame, I take into account the textual level of the dialogues which includes
Plato's motivations as an author of a literary work.

The Protreptic Function and Three Endoxical Premises

In this section, I briefly present three endoxical premises and discuss their
relation to Socrates' protreptic discourse. These premises are: (D) all
humans desire the good; (B) virtue is beneficial; and (T) virtue is like a
technē.[13] From this point forward, these premises are to be understood
in terms of their regulative role and are referred to simply as 'endoxical'
premises. They are fundamental to SM in two ways: (1) when taken in their
endoxical sense, they are the raw material for the elenctic and truth-seeking
functions; (2) when given a Socratic interpretation, they are the basis for the
protreptic function and they constitute the core argument for Socrates'
moral position. In this second capacity, the three premises are referred to
as 'protreptic' premises.

Premise (D) – all humans desire the good – is the eudaimonist principle that Socrates presupposes in SM which was discussed in Chapter 1. The truth of this belief is rarely disputed because it is taken to mean that people usually desire what they believe to be good. In its simplest form, Socrates treats the principle as uncontroversial and proposes it as such in the *Euthydemus* and *Lysis*. However, the premise often calls for clarification in some dialectical contexts since an important distinction must be made between the apparent good, for example what people think they desire, and the real good, for example what human beings, given their rational nature, really do desire. In the *Meno* (77b-78b), Socrates sets aside part of Meno's definition that virtue is the 'desire for what is honorable' (*epithumounta tōn kalōn*) and the ability to acquire it, by connecting what is honorable to what is good. Then, in a quick series of steps, he gets Meno to agree that the desire (*boulesthai*) for good 'belongs to our common nature' (78b8). The endoxical premise occupies an important part of the refutation of Protagoras (*Prt.* 358d; cf. 345e). The premise lends support to the Socratic prudential paradox: 'no one desires the bad', or goes towards what is painful, and the moral paradox: 'no one chooses or does injustice voluntarily'. Premise (D) also raises issues both about the nature of desire as a lack, with respect to what is desired, and the relation between goods, which are ranked on a scale of values with respect to what is good instrumentally and what is good for its own sake. In this context, the premise is relevant to the refutation of Polus (*Grg.* 467c-468e) and the discussion of the final good or first friend (*proton philon*) in the *Lysis* (219b-221d).

Premise (B) is virtue is beneficial (*ōphelimon*). The endoxical meaning of this premise is that being virtuous and doing virtuous actions furthers the agent's interests, where 'interests' are taken in an external sense, and 'virtue' is taken in a behavioral sense. Because virtuous action is not always in the agent's own interests, the premise may sometimes be taken to mean that the appearance of virtue is beneficial because it brings with it the rewards of a good reputation. In this regard, Premise (B) is coupled with a companion premise (B1): 'virtue is admirable' or 'fine' (*kalon*). The term 'beneficial' (*ōphelimon*) is often interchangeable with 'good' (*agathon*), and results in a popular expression which is used to speak highly of a virtuous man as *'noble and good' (kalos k'agathos)*.[14]

In both the *Lysis* (216c-d) and *Symposium* (204b-e), the object of love or desire is the 'beautiful' (*to kalon*), and the inference is made instantly, by Socrates, that what is beautiful is good (*to agathon*). Given Plato's sense of play with popular etymology, it follows that the occasion presents itself for Socrates to use the connection between good and beautiful in the refutation of Agathon (201c-d). This refutation brings to mind now a point of emphasis for future discussion. A great source for ambiguity in Greek moral terminology stems from the fact that the same word '*to kalon*', which translates in English as 'beautiful' or 'fine', also translates as 'noble' or 'admirable' and is thereby endowed with an important moral meaning; and likewise with the negative evaluative term '*to aischron*' as 'ugly', 'base' or 'shameful'.

Premise (B) and (B1) are major players in many elenctic arguments. It must be kept in mind that these terms often occur with their opposites in pairs, for example beneficial/harmful; good/bad; admirable/shameful. For instance, Protagoras admits that 'courageous men do not feel base fears' (*ouk aischrous phobous*, 360b2). With a standard move, Socrates argues from the contrary and asks, 'if not base (*aischra*), then it must be admirable' (*kala*)?, to which he gets assent; then, bringing admirable and good together, he asks 'if admirable (*kala*) then good (*agatha*)?'. Protagoras agrees and is well on his way to being refuted. An important concept associated with beneficial and good is 'use' or 'usefulness' (*chrēsis*); for something to be beneficial it must be put to use. Socrates will emphasize the connection: good things are beneficial only to the extent that they are used well. Premise (B) has enormous dialectical power, especially in the definitional dialogues, where the interlocutor's proposed definition of a virtue often fails because it is not compatible with this premise (cf. *Chrm.* 159c1-2, 160e-161a, 165d-e, 169a-b; *La.* 192c5-7, 193d-e; and *Rep.* I; also *Cr.* 48b; *Prt.* 349e-350b, 351b-c).[15] The protreptic reading of this premise, however, is understood internally, with respect to the good of the soul (*Grg.* 476e-477b). Socrates argues explicitly for the protreptic reading of what is beneficial (*Eud.* 278d-283b, and *Meno* 87d-89a), which I will discuss shortly.

Premise (T) – is virtue is like a *technē* – is a premise that is used implicitly. It is rarely disputed by the interlocutors because virtue or excellence of any kind is taken to be some kind of ability, either natural or learned, and this ability is judged with respect to a thing's function, whether it be a bow or a flute, a horse or dog, a doctor or a general, or simply a human being. However, the protreptic reading only becomes clear in the *Gorgias* where Socrates offers a definite set of criteria which separates his view of *technē* from the views of Gorgias and Polus, and from most other interlocutors, for example Critias, Hippias, Ion, Polemarchus, Protagoras. Usually, Socrates has no trouble with the frequent comparison of virtue with the arts and sciences, and this move always allows him to speak of virtue as some kind of knowledge or skill, without further explanation. The premise becomes problematic, however, due to an important qualification which Socrates recognizes but often ignores for purposes of the refutation. This qualification is due to the fact that any knowledge is a knowledge for opposites, that is, can be used for good or bad ends. Also, a problem is raised in the *Meno* and

Protagoras: if virtue is some kind of technical knowledge, then it can be taught; however it appears, at least to Socrates, that no one has learned how to be virtuous.[16] A great potential for verbal ambiguity resides in the key terms of all three premises because they generously allow for an endoxical reading and a protreptic reading.

Socratic Interlocutors

As the foregoing discussion was intended to show, there are complex logical relations between the endoxical premises, and equally complex semantic relations among the key evaluative terms, and a significant difference between how the premises and terms are understood by various interlocutors and Socrates in a given dialectical context. Based on the endoxical premises, Socrates works with standard patterns of inference and relies on two very familiar analogies: the comparison between virtue and *technē* (arts/crafts), and the comparison between the soul and body. The premises and issues regarding them are best addressed in the context in which they are raised and in connection to the interlocutors and their character attributes.

The way in which Socrates conducts his protreptic discourses varies with each interlocutor. Also, there are the welcomed differences that Plato creates in dramatic structure, dialectical context and presentation of philosophical ideas. In light of the variations, I make use of a rough distinction between two main types of interlocutors, sophistic and non-sophistic, and I place the interlocutors roughly into four smaller groups.[17] The purpose of this classification is to emphasize the role of the interlocutors and the various kinds of influence they have on SM. The classification is predicated on the idea that the personality of the interlocutor, his emotional reactions to Socrates and his attitude towards dialectical discussion affect the style of persuasion that Socrates will use. It is important to keep in mind that many of the interlocutors whom Plato represents in the dialogues, the *dramatis personae*, are linked closely to the actual people and their life histories in fifth- and early fourth-century Greece.[18]

Starting with the non-sophistic category, I include Charmides, Cleinias, Crito, Euthyphro, Hippocrates, Ion, Laches, Lysis, Nicias and Polemarchus; I would also add Adeimantus, Cebes, Glaucon, Phaedrus, Simmias and Theaetetus. Within the non-sophistic category of interlocutors, I distinguish between Group 1: those who are at a young and impressionable age, for example Charmides, Cleinias, Hippocrates, Lysis, Phaedrus and Theaetetus, who do not claim to have any expertise or formal knowledge, though they do have opinions, of course, and Group 2: those who do claim to have some formal knowledge or professional expertise, for example Agathon, Euthyphro, Ion, Laches, Meno, Nicias and Polemarchus.[19] Within the sophistic category, I distinguish between Group 3: the professional Sophists, such as Euthydemus, Dionysodorus, Gorgias, Hippias, Prodicus, Protagoras and Thrasymachus who teach or speak publicly and presumably take fees, and Group 4: the non-professional sophistic-like interlocutors who have negative responses to Socrates and maintain a contentious attitude in the conversation, for example Anytus, Callicles, Critias, Meletus and Polus.

My classification of interlocutors and the distinction I make between non-sophistic and sophistic interlocutors is based, to some extent, on what Socrates says, in the *Apology* (29e-30a), about how he treats those people who seem not to care about virtue and their souls, and those who claim that they do care and have virtue. One need only look at the dialogues, however, to find that Socrates' handling of the interlocutors is particularized. This particularity is what gives SM its personal touch and its *ad hominem* reputation; that is, it has both a positive and negative side. It is positive because Socrates is versatile and sensitive to the needs of each interlocutor. The general point is given attention in the context of a discussion with Phaedrus about the true art of rhetoric as it would be practiced by a dialectician (*Phdr.* 271a-272c). Among other things, this involves classifying kinds of speeches and different types of souls, and Socrates speaks about matching up 'the speeches and the souls' (*ta logōn te kai psuchēs*, 271b1-2).

The method has a negative side insofar as Socrates manipulates the interlocutors psychologically; he finds their weaknesses, draws upon their sense of shame and mocks them. The negative side of Socrates' personal interactions has a greater impact on the interlocutor's attitude towards the dialectic and affects the reader's perception of SM as well. It is no surprise that the negative side gets associated with the overall *ad hominem* approach to the argumentation. In any case, one should not expect that Socrates will interact with young men such as Cleinias or Lysis, as he interacts with the Sophists. The psychological profile of each character makes a big difference in Socrates' questioning, especially with those interlocutors who have a conventional viewpoint and the Sophists who express an ambivalent attitude towards the Athenian populace.

The classification is also relevant to the protreptic mode of discourse which includes rhetorical and dialectical techniques that are in keeping with the dramatic situation. It is unlikely that the Sophists are going to be persuaded by Socrates to take up philosophy as a way of life, so the arguments Socrates uses to refute them proceed along different lines. As I hope to show, not only the arguments but also the fallacies in the arguments are geared towards the character of the interlocutor. To illustrate the protreptic discourse in its simplest form, I choose among the easiest and most cooperative kind of interlocutors from Group 1.

Examples of Protreptic Discourse

'Exhortation' is the word we use in English to convey the sense of the Greek word '*protreptikos*' which means 'a turning towards', 'urging' or 'persuasion' ('to incline towards': *protrepto, Eud.* 307a2). Socrates uses a protreptic mode of discourse to urge his listeners to take up philosophy; to care for the values of wisdom and virtue and for the good of their souls. In other words: 'one ought to pursue wisdom' (*philosophēteon, Eud.* 288d7).

The classic example of protreptic discourse occurs with Cleinias in the *Euthydemus* (278d-283b; 288d-293a) where Socrates gives two demonstrations of a protreptic or hortatory argument. In the *Lysis*, too, there is a demonstration. Socrates agrees to show Hippothales how to talk to one's beloved (206c-d). As soon as he gets the chance, Socrates proceeds to question Lysis. Instead of flattering the boy, Socrates aims to humble him by making him aware of his deficiency with respect to wisdom (207d-211a). I briefly present the protreptic discourses with Hippocrates (*Prt.* 310b-314c), Charmides (*Chrm.* 154c-158c) and Crito in the *Crito*.

One obvious feature that is common to these cases is that the interlocutors are non-sophistic; they are willing to learn, sincere and are not resistant to Socrates' protreptic efforts. Socrates is not trying to refute their positions; his arguments are easier to follow though the concepts he presents are not unambiguous. There are important differences between the Socratic sense of a term used such as 'happiness' (*eudaimonia*) or 'beneficial', and the interlocutor's ordinary understanding of the term that will become clear in these few passages. In my analysis of these conversations, I am not concerned to give a full account of the arguments or the dialogues, and I treat some texts in more detail than others. My intention is to focus on the protreptic themes and main lines of reasoning which Socrates uses. After I present the passages, I explain why I believe these passages can be used to identify a distinct Socratic moral position.

The *Euthydemus*

In the *Euthydemus*, the brothers, Euthydemus and Dionsyodorus, are Sophists who claim to teach virtue to anyone for a fee. They accept Socrates' suggestion that those who can teach virtue can also persuade the reluctant pupil to care about virtue and wisdom (274d-275a). So, they agree to exhibit their skill and 'protrepticize' (*protrepsaite*) Cleinias who is a young man at a tender age in need of instruction to promote his becoming a good person (cf. 278c8). Socrates is familiar with Cleinias' character and his ability to handle questioning (275c). As a prime example of both direct and indirect protreptic, Socrates offers encouragement to Cleinias throughout the discussion (cf. 275d8-9).

The brothers refute Cleinias' answers to the question: who is it that learns, the wise or the ignorant?, regardless of which way he responds. Socrates, then, helps Cleinias to understand that the brothers are joking and making sport in order to initiate him into the mysteries of their discipline (277d-278d). Their initiation apparently involves getting Cleinias to recognize the 'correct use of words' (*peri onomatōn orthotētos*). The brothers equivocate in order to refute Cleinias, and Socrates explains that the bout of play was meant for Cleinias to realize the ambiguity of the word 'learning' or the expression 'to learn' (*manthanein*). The word can apply both to those who do not know and to those who do. Those who do not know 'learn' in the sense of acquiring knowledge they did not have. Those who do know have already learned, and so 'learn' applies to what they know and have acquired. Depending on how Cleinias responds, the brothers switch to the meaning of the term which will refute his answer.

This eristic style of debate is contrasted immediately with SM. Socrates offers to show the brothers how he exhorts another to pursue philosophy and care for virtue. He starts with an obvious question and asks Cleinias whether it is true that all men wish to prosper (278e2). Granting this, the next step he takes is to ask how does one achieve this state, and he suggests the conventional view that happiness consists in having 'many good things'. Among the good things, those which are commonly considered to be really good are enumerated: wealth, health, good birth, power and honor, and the virtues of temperance, courage, justice and wisdom are added in, with Cleinias' consent. The greatest of goods, good fortune, was temporarily left out, and Socrates suggests that to include good fortune would be to repeat the same good twice. 'Wisdom is presumably good fortune, even a child could see that' (279d9-10). Cleinias is puzzled at this last remark, so Socrates proceeds with an analogy to the crafts to show how wisdom and good fortune are the same thing. Socrates then proposes that wisdom is what causes men to be fortunate, but secures the necessary agreement simply by equating wisdom with infallibility of judgment.

After this gloss, the next series of steps leads to the premise that whatever goods one has must be beneficial (280c-d).[20] After invoking the craft analogy again, he secures the premise that the only truly beneficial thing is that which is used rightly. This means that the conventional goods are neither good nor bad, but 'if they are guided by ignorance, they are greater evils ... whereas if understanding and wisdom guide them, they are greater goods, but in themselves neither sort is of any worth' (281d-e). Since all humans want to be happy and happiness consists of goods, which are good only if one has the knowledge of how to use them, it follows that such knowledge is the only true good. The last step needed is that everyone ought to pursue wisdom (282a-b), and should not be ashamed to do honorably whatever it takes to get it. Cleinias accepts the claim that this wisdom is teachable (282c-d), and Socrates points out that Cleinias is committed to loving and pursuing wisdom himself. Cleinias follows the line of reasoning and is convinced that this is what he ought to do (282d1-3). Socrates suggests to the brothers that they can pick up where he left off and question Cleinias next as to what kind of wisdom is necessary to make one happy.

The second protreptic begins with Cleinias at 288d-290e, and switches to Crito, who is listening to Socrates' narrative and interrupts him because Crito cannot believe that Cleinias was capable of answering Socrates' questions so well. At 291b-293b, Socrates and Crito re-enact the conversation that had taken place earlier with Cleinias. The transition between interlocutors is very smooth and may have been designed to alleviate any further doubts the reader might share with Crito about Cleinias' ability. It may have also been designed to include Crito as the object of Socratic discourse since Crito is presented as looking for someone to teach virtue to his sons (272d-e; 306d-307a).

At 288d, Socrates continues to demonstrate to the brothers how to exhort someone and starts out by reminding Cleinias of their agreement that everyone ought to pursue wisdom. Socrates adds that the pursuit is the 'acquiring of knowledge' called philosophy. He asks Cleinias what kind of knowledge it is which benefits us, and this leads to a distinction between the knowledge of making and the knowledge of using (289c). When Socrates asks whether the art of generalship might be the knowledge they are looking for, Cleinias does not go along because the general does not know how to use the victory he has won. They finally come to the kingly art which fails to qualify for the art they are seeking because it seems to have no distinct subject matter. It might be the knowledge of how to make men good but it is difficult to specify what this knowledge consists in (292c-e). The second protreptic is a continuation of the first, and like many Socratic conversations, the argument, as a whole, appears to go nowhere. Socrates has led Cleinias (and Crito) only so far and then the inquiry ends aporetically. The knowledge of good turns out to have itself as its subject. So Socrates turns to the brothers for help, but instead of help, Euthydemus continues to demonstrate his eristic method using a different kind of fallacy, similar to equivocation, with the terms 'know' and 'knowing'.[21]

The brothers had claimed that they can teach virtue but only manage to confound Cleinias when they are asked to demonstrate their method. Socrates had requested that they try to persuade Cleinias that he ought to become their student because he will learn important things from them. What the brothers show is that there is nothing valuable to be learned from them.[22]

The *Lysis*

A look at the protreptic discourse in the *Lysis* (207e-210a) shows that happiness is the starting point as well. Socrates engages Lysis and leads him to see that he lacks the knowledge which will entrust him to his family and friends, and that without this knowledge he will not have the freedom he needs to be happy. The passage begins when Socrates supposes that Lysis' parents are fond of him and desire to see him happy, hence it seems that they allow him to do whatever he likes and never hinder him (207e). In fact, Lysis says his parents prevent him from doing many things. And although Lysis is a free person, he is controlled by the slave who takes him to school, and then must submit to his schoolmasters. Socrates asks Lysis what reason he thinks his parents have for preventing him from being happy, since 'you hardly do a single thing that you desire?'. 'It is because I am not yet of age, Socrates' (208e10). But there are other things Lysis' parents do not prevent him from doing, and Socrates wants to know why. Lysis sees the point and admits that it is not the coming of age, but understanding which determines what he is and is not allowed to do. A series of craft examples illustrates that those who are entrusted are the skilled.

In summary, Socrates says that 'the case stands thus: with regard to matters in which we become intelligent, every one will entrust us with them . . . whereas in all those which we have failed to acquire intelligence . . . everyone will do his utmost to obstruct us' (210b-c).[23] The passage ends by connecting the concept of wisdom to usefulness and goodness which become the object of *philia*, friendship or love. Socrates tells Lysis that if he becomes wise everyone will be his friend and be intimate (*oikeioi*) with him because he would be 'useful and good' (210d2). But if he does not, then neither his parents nor his intimates will be his friends. Lysis tries to get Socrates to repeat what he has been saying to his friend, Menexenus, who has just rejoined their company. Socrates refuses and tells Lysis that he should do it since he was paying such close attention. However, if Lysis forgets any part of the discussion that just took place when giving an account of it, Socrates says he is willing to go over it again with Lysis at another time (211a-b). Lysis is unwilling to recount the exchange, and asks Socrates if he would talk with Menexenus on some other topic; in fact, the language of debate and competition enter into the discourse at this point.

There is no refutation of the interlocutor or his thesis in this discussion, even though Lysis is made aware of his ignorance. Socrates hopes to persuade Lysis to seek wisdom by turning his attention to what he desires to possess, which potentially belongs to him by kinship to his parents, yet he cannot have due to his lack of knowledge. Socrates is leading Lysis to see that he is a lover or seeker of what is, in a sense, already given to him by nature, though he does not yet possess it. The theme of the relation of desire to the good as a type of kinship relation runs through the whole drama and provides the paradigm for the form of self-knowledge which Socrates seeks to instill in his interlocutors. In its simplest form here, it is to get Lysis to become aware of himself and his desires and to recognize his need for improvement. The protreptic process is intended to be a self-persuasive process. The rest of the dialogue explores the conventional meanings of '*philia*' and Socrates gradually reinterprets the concept until it comes to have a Socratic meaning.[24]

The Protreptic Discourse with Hippocrates

At *Protagoras* 311b, Socrates cross-examines Hippocrates who wants Socrates to introduce him to Protagoras, so that he may learn from the great Sophist. After questioning Hippocrates, using the crafts as a paradigm, Hippocrates admits that he would be ashamed to be thought of as a Sophist. With the help of Socrates' suggestion, Hippocrates agrees that he does not seek out Protagoras to become a Sophist, but to get a general education (*paideia*), which is appropriate for a private citizen (312a-b). Now Socrates wonders whether Hippocrates is aware that he is about to submit his soul for treatment to a Sophist without knowing what a 'Sophist' is. Hippocrates thinks he knows what a Sophist is, one who has knowledge of wise things, and who makes others clever speakers (312c-d). But these properties also apply to crafts like lyre-playing. What wise things do Sophists know, in particular, and on what subject do they make people clever speakers? (312e). Hippocrates is stumped by this question and admits *aporia* (312e10). He has a desire for knowledge and he thinks he can get it from Protagoras though he does not know what a Sophist is or does, and, in this sense, he has shown his ignorance.[25]

The protreptic discourse continues. Socrates cautions Hippocrates about the danger of entrusting his soul to the Sophist without knowing what it is he expects to learn, and further explains to him what it is that a Sophist really does. In Socrates' view a Sophist is 'a sort of merchant or dealer in provisions on which a soul is nourished' (313c4-7). Socrates points out that concerning the health of the body, Hippocrates would be eager to seek advice from the doctor or trainer, but with regard to his soul which he values 'much more highly' than his body, and given that it is upon his soul that all his affairs depend, whether it becomes 'better or worse', Hippocrates does not think twice about it (313a-b). Socrates does not question whether Hippocrates values his soul more than his body, but assumes this is true and admonishes Hippocrates for his neglect.

To emphasize the point further, Socrates continues with the body–soul analogy, applying the idea of nourishment to each. Hippocrates does not quite get the point, and he asks Socrates what the soul is nourished on. Socrates answers 'doctrines' (*mathēmasi*), just like those which the Sophist sells (313c9). Having compared the body and soul initially, and then ranked the value of each, Socrates expands on the difference between them with respect to the two kinds of nourishment. Hippocrates can test food before it is eaten. However, with doctrines he is at a far greater risk because the Sophists who sell these wares could be ignorant of their value (313d-e), and because he must take them directly into the soul without knowing whether they are good or bad. It is only if 'one happens to have a doctor's knowledge . . . but of the soul . . .' is it safe to expose oneself to a Sophist (313e3). If the soul takes in the teachings of the Sophist in ignorance, or before they are examined for their worthiness, the soul could be harmed (314a-b).

In this example, as in many cases where protreptic argument dominates the conversation, Socrates is trying to change the way the interlocutor thinks with respect to some impending action presented in the drama of the dialogue. It is clear that Socrates hopes to affect Hippocrates' attitude and actions, by bringing to his attention the serious dangers of what Hippocrates is about to do. The ultimate conclusion that Socrates argues for is the conclusion that Hippocrates ought to care for his soul.

The *Charmides*

In the *Charmides*, the importance of the body–soul analogy to the protreptic force of the method is central. Socrates is introduced to Charmides by Critias on the pretext that Socrates is someone who has a remedy to cure Charmides' headache (155b-c). At 156b-c, Socrates says he was in doubt as to what method he would use to demonstrate the power of the remedy, which consists of a leaf and a charm. The charm is not the kind of thing that can be used to cure the head in isolation from the rest of the body.

When Charmides indicates that he understands this idea, Socrates goes into a detailed explanation of the Zalmoxian medical practice which advocates a holistic approach, based on the relation between the body and soul. Socrates makes the analogy that 'just as one should not attempt to cure the eyes apart from the head, nor the head apart from the body, so one should not attempt to cure the body apart from the soul' (156e1-2, trans. Sprague). The relation between body and soul is not reciprocal, however, for Socrates goes on to say that the 'soul is the source both of bodily health and bodily disease for the whole man' (156e9-10). The way to cure the soul is with the charm. The charm consists of 'beautiful words'. The virtue of temperance (*sōphrosunē*) is introduced as the effect which these words produce. Socrates claims that once the soul has *sōphrosunē* the health of the head and body is easy to maintain (157b).

This entire explanation is a therapeutic metaphor for the Socratic conviction that health of the soul is prior to health of the body. The explanation is protreptic because it serves as a means of getting the boy to submit his soul to questioning in the way that a doctor would try to get his patient to submit his body to medical treatment (157b-d). The question of whether Charmides already has *sōphrosunē* in his soul or not is raised. Since Charmides does not feel comfortable answering yes or no to this question, Socrates suggests that they inquire into the matter together, so that Charmides is not forced to say yes or no without further consideration, and Socrates does not have to administer his medicine without knowing which is the case. In order to decide the case, Socrates asks Charmides if he is willing to express his opinion about *sōphrosunē*. The series of refutations begins with Charmides' first attempt at a definition (159b-c). As with Cleinias, Lysis and Hippocrates, Charmides does not have a thesis to defend from the start. Socrates leads the conversation up to the point where the interlocutor's opinion is encouraged and elicited. In these four conversations, Socrates is portrayed as exercising a strong influence on the nature and direction of the discussion, and appears to be comfortable in this role. He is not portrayed as someone who meets an interlocutor who has a position to defend, and then proceeds to refute the interlocutor through a series of arguments in the search for a moral truth. Furthermore, in this case, Socrates is presented as a healer who has a therapeutic method which he uses in an effort to help the interlocutor to care for his soul.

The *Crito*

The Socratic principle set down in the *Crito* (47a) is that it is by knowledge that one should decide matters of great importance (cf. *La.* 184e). Socrates and Crito agree that they ought to take advice about important matters from the man who knows, and not worry about what the majority think in making a decision. He who disobeys such advice with respect to the body harms himself and likewise the soul, which is given priority of value over the body. Instead of using the word 'soul', Socrates asks Crito if that which suffers injustice is more valuable (48a-b), and whether the most important thing is not life but good life (48b-c). Before they begin the inquiry into whether it is right or wrong for Socrates to escape prison, Socrates tells Crito of his desire to persuade him, 'I am anxious to act in this matter with your approval, and not contrary to your wishes' (48e6–7).

Socrates presents Crito with some of the simplest and strongest arguments for his moral position based on the concepts of justice and harm using rational principles which he and Crito both accept, and yet Crito is not persuaded. Though Crito is a friendly interlocutor who loves Socrates and would like to believe him, Socrates is unable to persuade Crito in a straightforward manner. It takes the strong rhetoric and authority of the impersonal Laws to get the ideas across.

Conclusion: Protreptic Themes and Arguments

The central protreptic themes revolve around the desire for happiness, the priority of goods and the care for the soul, the moral virtues, and the knowledge required to care for the soul. One unifying perspective on these themes which is relevant to SM is the view that dialectical inquiry increases self-knowledge and self-knowledge is the way to care for the soul. Since dialectical activities are equated with seeking wisdom and doing philosophy, the exhortation to philosophy is the same old familiar tune that echoes in the ears of Socrates' most avid listeners.

I conclude with a brief overview. In most of the protreptic conversations, Socrates relies on one or more of the three endoxical premises. The significance of this set is noteworthy because when these premises are Socratically reinterpreted, they become protreptic premises in a protreptic argument. For each of the three premises, there is an endoxical and a protreptic interpretation.

By a 'protreptic argument', in general, I mean an argument which advocates the pursuit of wisdom, or promotes the good of the soul. An 'indirect protreptic argument' is a protreptic argument embedded in an elenctic argument. By a 'protreptic premise', I mean a premise that has been Socratically reinterpreted, which the interlocutor would be inclined to accept if he had self-knowledge. In the arguments he constructs, Socrates relies upon but does not accept the *prima facie* truth of the regulative endoxical premises. Instead, he changes the meaning of the premise to an interpretation which he thinks best explains the truth value of the premise, and in so doing, he transforms an endoxical premise into a protreptic premise, which supports the Socratic moral position.

The first premise is (D) all humans desire the good. The endoxical meaning of this premise is that everyone wants and pursues the 'apparent' good, or what they think are good things. The protreptic meaning is that everyone desires what is really good, regardless of what they think is good. The truth of this protreptic premise supports the Socratic paradox that no one desires what is bad or does wrong voluntarily.

The second premise is (B) virtue is beneficial. The endoxical meaning of this premise is that being virtuous and doing virtuous actions furthers one's self-interest, taken in an external sense. Because virtue is not always in one's self-interest nor is it directly beneficial, the premise may sometimes be taken to mean that the appearance of virtue is always beneficial. As I noted earlier, the protreptic meaning is that virtue is always beneficial for the soul. The truth of this protreptic premise supports the Socratic values of justice and virtue, for these are the qualities which are most beneficial for the soul to possess. I discuss the significance of premise (B) by contrasting Socrates' view of harm and benefit with the conventional view of Polemarchus in the next chapter.

The third premise is (T) virtue is like a *technē*. The endoxical meaning is that doing anything well requires skill or expertise. The ordinary reasoning is that if virtue is equated with doing well in the political and social realms, then virtue is a kind of expertise. When this premise is Socratically reinterpreted, it lends support to Socrates' belief in the value of moral knowledge, and underlies the Socratic paradox that virtue is knowledge.

Chapter 3

Ambiguity and Argumentation

Introduction

My overall project is to show that understanding SM contextually, within the framework of the drama, makes good sense of Socrates' practice since the argumentation actually works with the character types and situations being presented. My interest in ambiguity is part of this project, for I think that the fallacy of equivocation and other dialectical tactics are related specifically to the details of the drama, for example the themes or issues as they are presented in the dialogue and the *ad hominem* aspects of the argumentation. Ambiguity is useful for two purposes. The first use is from the internal frame of the dialogue, at the dramatic level. Socrates uses verbal ambiguity as a strategic device. He can work freely within a wide range of meanings and draw out conceptual connections which allow him to refute the interlocutor and to put together a protreptic argument. He can take a real difference of opinions between himself and the interlocutor, and by virtue of the words and ideas involved in the exchange, collapse the differences in meaning, either by showing how the interlocutor's notion is related to his or by outright substitution.

The second use is from the external frame, at the textual level. Ambiguity is a versatile literary device. It serves Plato's purpose as a dramatist who wishes to portray lifelike representations of action and thought between characters in dialogue with each other. But there is not only this; there is also a conflict of ideas, and opposing arguments are being proposed and rejected. As a philosopher, Plato is interested in the problems of language use and misuse, and how language maps on to or represents reality. Both literary and philosophical purposes merge together and are made manifest to the readers by Plato's art. So then, the problems he is grappling with include the concept of meaning, the lack of clarity in expression, the diversions of rhetorical and poetic language which entertain rather than instruct, intentional obscurity, irony, etymology, puns, multiple meaning and definition.

Plato's portrayal of ambiguity in the dialogues also serves a pedagogical purpose, for it requires readers to recognize that more than one meaning is at play in the discourse and it challenges them to follow more than one path in the reasoning. Readers are invited to see two sides of the story, compare meanings and watch how a single word or phrase can interfere with understanding. Plato shows both dramatically and through argumentation how serious the need is to make proper distinctions between the meanings of key terms. The reader is not only being asked to recognize the problems of language use but to disambiguate and resolve the difficulties. The use of ambiguity in argumentation belongs to the dramatic action taking place between speakers. Once one makes the connections between the use of ambiguity and other fallacies in the argumentation, and the attributes of the characters, their interactions and the philosophical themes, the chances are that this will effectively change how one understands the dynamics of the dialogues.

I argue that the method should be conceived and interpreted dramatically. I present SM fully within its dialectical context which includes strong adversarial positioning, animated debates, muddled conversations, backtracking, role reversals, rhetorical speeches, appeals to emotion and the deliberate misinterpretations of meaning. Plato uses boxing, wrestling and battle imagery to convey the rough and tumble action associated with the arguments which often have an offensive or defensive tone. My interpretation of SM requires that it be seen as functioning in more than one way at the same time; the three modes of discourse are operating together sometimes very loosely, and it might seem that Socrates is a type of juggler tossing up and moving around discourses as in a performative act. Perhaps. But when SM is seen as a three-way activity rather than from one standpoint, for example the standpoint of inquiry into truth by search for definition, or the standpoint of the *elenchos* as it has been narrowly circumscribed, one gains a valuable perspective on the diverse tactics and style of philosophy as Socrates practices it, and as Plato portrays it in full dramatic dress. This perspective derives from aesthetic appreciation; it is a consummate interest that nurtures an attitude towards philosophy and keeps one's mind fertile and open.

My approach offers advantages in terms of explaining why there are fallacies in the arguments and what kind of fallacies there are. The arguments are tricky and do not meet the formal standards of logic, but this does not mean they are without merit. The advantage comes in seeing how the fallacies and problematic moves can be interpreted protreptically if the dramatic context is worked into the argumentation that Socrates uses, including most of all the ambiguities of language, and the customization of argument to the interlocutor's character.

One of the major drawbacks of SM, from my point of view, is that the elenctic and epistemic functions are at cross-purposes. They have different immediate aims and follow a different set of rules for how to achieve that aim. Though all three functions have a single moral aim, there is a problem with mixing these functions together; to put the point bluntly: Socrates is playing by two sets of rules which come into conflict on many occasions. I will come back to this difficulty in the next chapter. To conclude this section, there is one more point of difficulty I will raise now and return to in the next chapter.

The dialogues show that Socrates is committed to truth and is intent on getting the interlocutor to give an account of his beliefs. Socrates sometimes goes to great lengths to establish the need for an inquiry and to get it going on the right track, in a friendly way. The cross-questioning is conducted within a conceptual framework provided by Socrates who steers the inquiry from start to finish, and yet he acts like a fool who is in the dark searching for what is right in front of him. This strikes a sour note with most readers. SM involves ironic pretense on Socrates' part; he covers his serious moral intentions with a comic mask. In the drama of the dialectic, one watches Socrates engage in dissembling and very distasteful conduct.

To ameliorate the tensions or negative feelings that this behavior causes, one should mark how many times Plato has Socrates mock himself as well as his interlocutor, and take note of how aware he is of his proximity to the eristic or combative style of debate. I also recommend that readers read the 'middle-to-later' dialogues, for example *Symposium*, *Phaedrus*, *Cratylus*, and *Theaetetus*, which capture the same spirit of Socrates but in a less abrasive and annoying manner.[1] Socrates' constant awareness of his limitations is dramatically related to the persistent Platonic theme of philosophy as a form of *erōs*, a natural desire in the soul for what is good that all humans experience and ought to pursue rationally. I think enough has been said about the particular aims and activities of the elenctic and protreptic functions; however, there is a gap to be filled with respect to the epistemic function.

The Epistemic Function

As part of the epistemic mode of discourse, Socrates makes an 'essentialist' assumption, which holds that to grasp the meaning of a concept of a thing, one must look for a common quality or form which each thing shares with all other things of its kind. This supposed commonality makes it possible to state the essence (*ousia*), or give a definitional account (*logos*) of the concept in question. The essentialist assumption is what underlies the familiar Socratic question about the virtues: what is it? (*ti esti*). Socrates seeks the essence of a virtue and distinguishes its essence from an accidental quality (*poion*) that happens to be true of it (*pathos ti*, e.g. *Eu.* 6d-e). There is usually a distinctive approach which he takes to the definitional question relative to the drama of a dialogue. In the *Meno*, he puts the question, 'what is virtue?', and asks for a description in terms of a single form (*eidos*) that is the same in all cases (72c6–7). In the *Laches*, Socrates speaks of the power (*dunamis*) which makes a courageous man be courageous (192b7), and in the *Charmides*, Socrates asks Charmides to look into his soul (*psuchē*) for the presence of temperance (*sōphrosunē*) so he can better explain what it is (159a1-2).

For Socrates, the what-is-it question is useful because by means of it, he can specify certain standards for a definition which are both descriptive and normative. In my view, his reason for putting so much emphasis on definitional meanings is not because he wishes to learn about a moral concept descriptively or to know how a term is ordinarily used (his irony is misleading in this context); rather, he seeks to establish what a concept *ought* to mean and how a term *ought* to be used given a set of ethical ideals to which one is committed.

The Socratic activity of looking for universal definitions is part of the search for knowledge, but it is also a dialectical activity designed to promote an attitude towards philosophical inquiry. Socrates' dialectical arguments are built around normative definitions that are based on a set of values which he wishes to offer to the interlocutors for their consideration, as an alternative to their own conceptions which he tries to dismantle. I suggest that when Socrates trades on an ambiguity he really is trying to exchange one meaning for another with the hope that his meaning will help to resolve the conflicts between the interlocutor's set of beliefs, which the Socratic elenctic magnifies by asking leading questions and exposing verbal or logical inconsistencies.

The various efforts to define the virtues end in *aporia*. These efforts, however, begin with the deceptively simple and naïve notion that a proper formulation of piety or courage can be found and put into so many words, and then Socrates, the interlocutors, their listeners and the participant readers could be done with it and get on with the business of life. Fortunately, this is not how it works. Looking for the defining features of a moral concept which one habitually relies upon in making common evaluative judgments, and failing to find such features, is one of the dramatically compelling ways for Plato to show that there is a persistent problem with the meaning of ordinary words and established usage. While the epistemic function of SM is fueled by the search for meaning, the underlying question that one is left with is whether words, given in any sort of formulaic account, are enough to capture the ideas that they are meant to describe.

Instead of resolving the questions raised in the dialogues, Socrates and the interlocutors are trapped in the nets of language and need to tackle a series of verbal distinctions upon which the entire success of the conversation depends. Once the conventional meanings of moral concepts are disrupted and challenged, the interlocutor, as well as the reader, may tend to view the rest of the inquiry process as so much pettifogging and silly nonsense, a waste of time sitting around exchanging words. This attitude is confirmed by unredeemable interlocutors like Thrasymachus, Critias and Callicles, as they are caught in what appears to them to be nothing more than logical traps.[2] In the *Symposium*, Alcibiades complains loudly about the pitfalls and frenzies of philosophical discussion (*te kai bakcheias*, 218b4). A similar negative attitude towards Socratic-style babbling (*adoleschia*) is dramatized by Aristophanes through the comic actions of *The Clouds* (1479-85) and in the last refrain of *The Frogs* (cf. *Phd.* 70c1-4; *Phdr.* 269e-270a; *Tht.* 195b-c; *Crat.* 401b8).

> Right it is and befitting,
> Not, by Socrates sitting,
> Idle talk to pursue,
> Stripping tragedy-art of
> All things noble and true.
> Surely the mind to school
> Fine-drawn quibbles to seek,
> Fine-set phrases to speak,
> Is but the part of a fool![3]

For a quick reminder, Socrates refutes Agathon all too swiftly by trading on the conceptual connections between beautiful and good (*Sym.* 201a-d). Having agreed that (1) love lacks beauty, Socrates presses Agathon on whether (2) good things are beautiful and he agrees; Socrates concludes that (3) love lacks goodness. Premise (2) is semantically ambiguous. If good things have an essential, not just an accidental, connection with beauty (which is a hard case to prove), then the conclusion follows, but if beauty is an accidental property of goodness (which is easier to demonstrate since some good things are not beautiful), then the argument is invalid (cf. *HMaj.* 297c-d).

The *Symposium* is a good example to mention on the topic of truth and definitions since each speaker takes himself to know who or what love (*erōs*) is and praises love profusely without being clear what they mean by the term. The inability to get at the meaning which most of Socrates' interlocutors take themselves to grasp with no trouble provides an initial clue about the need for the persuasive speech and literary devices Socrates and Plato use and why we, as readers, can't simply eliminate them from SM. The devices of narrative reports, retelling of myths, poetically vivid imagery, ironic humor, incessant puns, analogies, metaphors and other figures of speech are not extraneous to the arguments, but show something crucial about the effort of Socrates and the interlocutors to find the truth by means of language and their seeming inability to get beyond the limits of language. The fact is that they cannot be done with the inquiry and get on with life. Plato dramatizes the plight of the philosopher and the ordinary man who together try to find the right words to express their ideas, but who are none the less at odds with each other about the meaning of the words they use. Due to what is an inevitable misunderstanding that occurs between them, there is a mild but looming sense of tragedy. This sense of tragedy is due to the unavoidable miscommunication that occurs between people when they disagree with each other about what an idea means or what to call something, especially with regard to serious actions and matters of principle. Ambiguity in speech and the misinterpretation of meaning show up in the tragic conflicts and dramatized, agonistic debates (*agōnes*) between Creon and Antigone, for instance, or Phaedra and the Nurse, Hippolytus and his father, or Teucer and the sons of Atreus.[4] Such misinterpretation of meaning and the antagonism it generates is called 'tragic ambiguity'. Tragic drama is a suitable artistic medium for displaying the range of differences that exist between people who perceive and describe the same situation in opposing ways.

Simon Goldhill argues that the experience of irresolvable opposition which is expressed in tragedy is rooted in every aspect of the Greek intellectual tradition in Socrates' heyday. Antagonism exists in Greek mythology, as the poets reveal, in political debates as conveyed by Thucydides; it provides the subject matter of rhetorical displays and set pieces given by the Sophists. Both Protagoras and Antiphon had a reputation for their expertise in composing speeches of opposing *logoi* that could be delivered in the courtroom. The Presocratics, such as Heraclitus and Zeno, grappled with paradox and the profundity or frivolity of contradictory predicates. In a similar vein, Plato is concerned with internal psychological conflict and social disunity. Plato's dialogues represent the conflict of ideas and arguments which Socrates explores, using these same patterns of 'polarity and reversal'. Goldhill sees this phenomenon not merely as a 'surface effect' arising from the embellishments of language and idle theorizing, but as a serious philosophical concern about the nature of social and physical reality.[5]

My objective in this chapter is to explain the nature and purpose of the ambiguity and other dialectical strategies in SM. I shall claim that Plato is effectively dramatizing the problems of miscommunication associated with the ambiguity of language in ordinary discourse. Socrates plays out this activity to the hilt in ways that are humorous and serious. Plato has Socrates go to tedious lengths to show that it is only by being clear on the meaning of the words being used that progress in how we think about things can be made. Seldom is the problem of language made explicit, but this is what the dramatic action shows us. I think a red flag goes up as soon as the questioning turns on what the interlocutors mean and how they conceive of what they are saying. In real life as in literature, ambiguity and irony are effective tools because they allow a speaker or writer to convey more than one thing at the same time which then may be contrasted with each other in meaning. To show Plato's consuming concern with language and methods of communication, I turn briefly to the *Phaedrus*. I explain my motivation for doing so after the exposition of the passage (261a-266c).

A Detour to the *Phaedrus*

There is a protreptic episode between Socrates and Phaedrus, both of whom are self-described and dramatized as lovers of discourse. As usual, Socrates specializes in showing human beings their deficiencies in exactly the area that they most want to become proficient. Phaedrus wants to become an artful speaker and cultivate a style of eloquent and persuasive speech. He imitates the style of Lysias, a prominent rhetor and speechwriter; he hopes to learn the techniques of rhetoric and studies rhetorical handbooks; but when he imitates the orators and recites the speeches, he does so without regard for the quality of their moral content. Socrates attempts to bring Phaedrus around to seeing the need to study philosophy as part of his training because, as he will argue, philosophy is part of the art of speaking. This entails giving one's attention to the content as well as the composition of the speech and the way the language is used.

In this scene, Socrates brings forth arguments with the inspiration he receives from the Muses and nymphs in the area. Addressing them as 'noble creatures', he calls on them asking them to 'persuade the fair young Phaedrus that unless he pay proper attention to philosophy he will never be able to speak properly about anything' (261a4–8). Socrates tries to persuade Phaedrus that a student of rhetoric must seek the truth about the nature and order of things (*ta onta*) and use language carefully and responsibly. In fact, the point is stronger; it is only by turning one's attention to the things that words are about that words are used correctly, and this attention is what enables one to speak well.

In a well-known passage, Socrates defines rhetoric as an 'art which leads the soul by means of words (*technē psychagōgia tis dia logōn*), not only in law courts and the various other public assemblages, but in private companies as well' (261a8-10, cf. 271d1-2). Phaedrus has a narrower understanding of what rhetoric is and does, and he thinks the term applies only to public speaking and politics. Socrates appeals to the Homeric heroes, such as Nestor and Odysseus, as examples of men who speak nobly and privately, and alludes to their real life counterparts, whom, as Phaedrus is made to guess, are the Sophists, Gorgias and Thrasymachus. Such artful speakers are also artful debaters who can make the 'same thing appear to the same persons at one time just and at another, if he wishes, unjust' (261d1-2). Adding Zeno of Elea to his list, Socrates refers to those who specialize in *antilogikē*, which is the ability to argue both sides of a case equally well. This skill is associated with Protagoras and put to eristic use, as the brothers haplessly display in the *Euthydemus*, but it need not be so used. Socrates, as the proto-dialectician, is the one who knows how to use these abilities.

The 'antilogicists' or 'logic-choppers' are deceivers in argument who are able to deceive best when the topics they discuss, the just and the unjust, and the terms used in speaking on such topics, appear to resemble each other and are difficult to distinguish. Only those who really know the truth and pursue such matters earnestly have an art, and only they can speak correctly or lead others rightly. The rest of those who pretend to be skillful speakers and debaters pursue nothing but opinion and are ridiculous (*geloian*, 262c). Phaedrus gives an unenthusiastic response to all this until Socrates suggests they look at Lysias' speech and compare it critically with the speeches given by Socrates, which just happen, by a stroke of good luck, 'to contain an example of how someone who knows the truth can mislead his audience by playing a joke on them in the course of his speech' (262d1-4, trans. Waterfield).

Phaedrus reads a few lines from Lysias' speech. Socrates begins his critique and asks, 'It is clear to everyone that we are in accord about some matters of this kind and at variance about others, is it not?' (263a4-6). Phaedrus assents but asks for an explanation. Socrates makes the point, similar to but not exactly like the one he makes to Euthyphro. The topics of piety and justice, right and wrong, are the cause of trouble among the gods rather than matters of number and counting, weights and measures (*Eu.* 7b-d). In this case, Socrates asks about words: when someone uses words like 'iron' or 'silver', people have the same understanding but if someone uses words such as 'justice' and 'goodness', then people are at odds with each other and with themselves (263b6-9). It is about the disputed or 'doubtful things' (*tōn amphisbētēsimōn*, 263c7-8) that people have so much confusion and are so easily deceived, and amongst such things is the word 'love' about which Lysias had written his speech and which he failed to define. Socrates asks

Phaedrus to remind him whether in his first speech he had defined love. Phaedrus said that he had, and, as it turns out, Socrates treated the subject methodically like the true speech-lover should (237b-238d).

In his first speech on love, Socrates provided a corrective to how others usually approach such subjects and explained the general pattern which he takes, in a way that is similar to Diotima's speech (*Sym.* 201d-212b). This pattern captures the structure of SM in its simplest form. He sets out to address the question, as posed by Lysias' speech, as to whether it is better for the loved one to prefer and grant sexual favors to a non-lover rather than to his lover. Socrates explains, 'let us first agree on a definition of love, its nature and its power, and then, keeping this definition in view and making constant reference to it, let us enquire whether love brings advantage or harm' (237d1-5). So, he follows his own advice and defines the meaning of love initially, in broad terms, saying in his usual way, 'Now everyone sees that love is a desire', and continues from there.

As part of his critique of Lysias, Socrates is summarizing the content of his first speech. He had separated two kinds of madness: human and divine, and then looking to divine madness, he distinguished love from the other three kinds: prophecy, mystical madness and poetic madness, each belonging respectively to Apollo, Dionysus and the Muses, with love belonging to Aphrodite and Erōs (265b-c). Going back to his description of the new art of rhetoric, Socrates had briefly suggested a methodological division (*hodō dierēsthai*) which would sort out the disputed or doubtful terms of a discussion from the non-disputed terms (263b7). He now explains how he followed two methodological principles in his first speech: one principle brings all the particulars together to form a definition of one class of things, and by means of this principle, Socrates says, his speech 'acquired clearness and consistency' (265d8); the other principle divides among the one class of things two branches which share the same name (*hōmonuma*, 266a1, 10) and these are sorted out by further differences. This is the method of 'collecting and dividing' things, of which this Socrates, the Socrates of the *Phaedrus*, professes to be a lover (266b4). Such a man who knows how to use the method in discussion he calls a 'dialectician', not knowing whether this is quite the right name for him or not (266c1).

The *Phaedrus* lends credibility to the idea that Plato puts the dramatic spotlight on how two speakers fail to communicate in spite of themselves because they are using the same word to mean different things. In my view, Plato intends to raise the reader's awareness of ambiguity to a higher level to show the need to define one's terms clearly and make appropriate distinctions. Though the method Plato explains here, and elsewhere, may seem like so much dry, doctrinal theorizing at the abstract level, the Socratic life of philosophical conversation which takes place at the practical level is the method's best instantiation. Plato's Socrates' pursuit of precise meaning and correct language is illustrated with both the Sophists and the conventional interlocutors but this occurs at different levels of intensity, for it is the Sophists and rhetoricians who capitalize on the misuse of words and profit from showy argumentation.

The section I have just exposited from the *Phaedrus* continues in a protreptic mode with a comparison of the body to the soul, for example, just as those who practice the art of medicine must understand the nature of the body holistically to treat it properly, so too must those who intend to study or practice the art of rhetoric must understand the nature of the soul. There is a parallel passage where Socrates of the *Charmides* urges a similar approach (156d-157c). As part of his advocacy to a holistic approach to the study of the soul (270b-e), Socrates of the *Phaedrus* spells out the connection between the art of dialectic as rhetoric and a program in which a dialectician is obligated to improve the souls of his audience by properly investigating the nature of the soul and customizing his speech to the needs of a particular respondent (271a-272c). Going further into the topic would take me too far afield, but I wish to emphasize that it is essential to an adequate study of SM to adopt a perspective that looks into a range of dialogues, some of which show Plato's explicit concern with method, language and the soul.

I take the viewpoint that the Socratic and Platonic methodology in the corpus is continuous and unified. I do not find any basis for thinking that an 'earlier' method was abandoned and replaced with a 'later' method, such as the method of hypothesis, in conformity to a chronological group of dialogues.[6] Eventually, Plato does limit the role of the *elenchos* in later dialogues and recognizes the drawbacks of the harsh, *ad hominem* side of eristic style of discourse.[7] For the most part, Plato's innovations in dialectical method are cumulative; his conception of philosophy is rational discourse or 'dialectic' broadly understood. I find that Plato is always concerned with a model of knowledge that is rooted in dialectical knowledge. This model involves knowing how to put things to good use (*Eud.* 290c-d; *Crat.* 390c-d; *Rep.* VII 510c-511e; *Phil.* 16b-c). The dialectician knows how to put to good use the language, definitions, arguments, sciences and all the other things of philosophy as they are experienced in practical life. The method of hypothesis and the method of division are referred to as 'dialectic'. Various versions are described or demonstrated in the *Phaedo* (99e-100b; 101d-e), *Republic* (531c-534e), *Philebus* (15d-18d), *Sophist* and *Statesman*. In these texts as well as the *Phaedrus*, dialectic has both a technical and a broader meaning, and involves Plato's ontological commitments to essences or Forms, or to the doctrine of recollection.

Ambiguity

'Ambiguity' refers to the presence of two or more possible meanings and may apply either to a word or to a sentence. Ambiguity in a single word is called 'lexical', 'linguistic' or 'verbal' ambiguity, or, more technically, 'homonymy', and it indicates that the same word can have several senses. The majority of words have more than one sense, but they are not considered ambiguous primarily because the context serves to disambiguate the word. A word is 'ambiguous' when it is used ambiguously, that is, when it is difficult to know which meaning is being used in a particular instance, and the context is not sufficient to disambiguate the meanings.[8] Because most words have more than one sense, it is the use of a word in a sentence, or the sentence itself, that is properly called 'ambiguous'. Deciding whether a word is being used ambiguously requires careful consideration of contextual factors and facets of communication, such as the rest of the words in the sentence, where and when the sentence is uttered, what previous sentences were uttered, to whom the sentence is uttered, and the background knowledge about the speaker; it cannot be determined by looking at the word itself. Ambiguity in a sentence may be caused either by a semantic or a syntactic ambiguity. A syntactic ambiguity or 'amphiboly' is due to the grammatical construction of a sentence. With respect to the distinction between these two types of ambiguity, I am concerned, in general, with semantic and not syntactic ambiguity.

Whenever I discuss the ambiguous use of language, I talk about the meanings of words and sentences which signify concepts and the relation these concepts have to each other and to the things they represent. With regard to the terms and premises in an argument, I am concerned with the 'pragmatics' of meaning which involves the use of language to convey the *intended* meaning of the speaker to the listener in a conversational context, and not with the dictionary or literal meaning of a word. I am not concerned with the linguistic description or the etymological meaning of words, and their uses in sentences, nor am I concerned with the formal problems of ambiguity as a natural or inherent phenomenon of language. The ambiguity that I am concerned with has to do with language use, and how it affects and enhances Socratic argumentation.

The words 'ambiguity' and 'equivocation' are closely related and are sometimes used interchangeably. They are synonymous when they are used to indicate that a single word has more than one meaning. However, I believe it is best to distinguish between 'ambiguity' and 'equivocation' because the concept of 'ambiguity' is broader. By 'equivocation', I refer to a fallacy (invalid argument) that is due to the ambiguity of a term, where that term is used in more than one sense in the premises or conclusion of an argument. In a valid argument, the same terms must have the same meaning if the conclusion is to follow from the premises.

In my discussion of Socrates' use of ambiguity, I clarify how I think an expression is intended by Socrates, and specify what I think is the likely interpretation given to that expression by the interlocutor. In determining how a premise is being interpreted, it is helpful to consider the semantic meaning, or truth value, of that premise from the perspective of both the speaker and listener. The semantic meaning that is given to a premise refers to whether Socrates or his interlocutor considers the premise true or false. The semantic ambiguity of a premise indicates that a premise can be interpreted in more than one way simultaneously, that is, either it is true under one interpretation and false under another, or it may be true under both interpretations but for different reasons. The three regulative endoxical premises, identified in Chapter 2, are semantically ambiguous premises. Other examples are 'great power is a good thing', and 'it is better to err voluntarily than involuntarily'. Both Socrates and his interlocutors agree that such premises are true, yet they assign different meanings to the premises and to the terms. Within the specific context of argumentation, I am chiefly concerned with Socrates' use of semantic ambiguity. Since the main reason why a premise is semantically ambiguous is due to the ambiguity of the terms that are used in that premise, I am primarily concerned with the double meaning of the terms that Socrates makes use of in constructing his arguments.

Terminology

Socrates and the interlocutor are engaged from start to finish in the activity of trying to figure out what the interlocutor means by a term and its corresponding concept.[9] The interlocutor is a conventional thinker who uses a commonly shared language base as any speaker would in an ordinary conversation. The Sophists, however, are a special case for they understand the transforming power of words and are gifted in poetic speech. When Socrates poses questions, he is particularly concerned with the meanings that the interlocutor attaches to four categories of terms.

These categories are: (i) the terms which refer to value: 'virtue' (*aretē*), 'good' (*agathon*), 'bad' (*kakon*), 'beneficial' (*ōphelimon*), 'harmful' (*blaberon*), 'use' (*chrēsis*), 'useful' (*chrēsimos*), 'admirable' (*kalon*), 'shameful' (*aischron*), 'happiness' (*eudaimonia*) and 'misery' (*kakodaimonia*); (ii) the terms which refer to motivation: 'want', 'desire' or 'wish' (*epithumein* or *boulesthai*), 'love' (*erōs*), 'voluntary' (*hekōn*) and 'involuntary' (*akōn*); (iii) the terms which refer to a capacity or to the product of a capacity: 'work' or 'function' (*ergon*), 'power' (*dunamis*), 'true' (*alēthēs*), 'false' (*pseudēs*) and 'persuasion' (*peithos*); and (iv) the terms which refer to knowledge: 'skill' (*technē*), 'wisdom' (*sophia* or *phronēsis*), 'knowledge' or 'understanding' (*epistēmē* or *gignōskein*).

In the definitional dialogues, the interlocutor is usually prompted to propose an initial thesis concerning the definition of a moral concept. The key terms, to be added to the first category, are the specific virtues of 'courage' (*andreia*), 'holiness/piety' (*to hosion/eusebeia*), 'justice' (*dikaiosunē*), 'temperance' (*sōphrosunē*) and their respective opposites. In these cases, Socrates questions the interlocutor and persists in clarifying the meaning of a given term. However, with regard to the terms that are contained in the regulative endoxical premises, Socrates usually allows the meaning that the interlocutor has in mind to prevail without questioning. When Socrates persists in clarifying the meaning of a term in a proposed thesis, he is not concerned with the finer terminological quibbles or with the etymology of words, as Prodicus is, nor with fixing a particular meaning from the start of the inquiry; rather, he is interested in getting the interlocutor to be clear about what he wants to say and to stick by that meaning of the term during the refutation.[10] This is not an easy thing to get the interlocutor to do because often the interlocutor is not sure exactly what he means. At times, the interlocutor's response is treated like a riddle (*ainigmati*) that must be solved, for example Charmides' definition of temperance as 'doing one's own business' (161b8), Polemarchus' citation of Simonides' saying that justice is 'to render to each his due' (*Rep.* I 331e2-4).

Making the Meaning Clear

At times, Socrates does not make it clear that he takes something the interlocutor says differently than the interlocutor takes it himself, even though it is apparent that Socrates realizes this. For instance, Socrates switches to a different meaning of a term without acknowledging the difference with Critias (*Chrm.* 165b-c). Using the Delphic maxim 'Know thyself' as the source of his view, Critias defines temperance as knowing (*gignōskein*) oneself (164d-165b). Socrates takes a moment to reply and says that if temperance is knowing (*gignōskein*) anything then it must be knowledge (*epistēmē*) of something. This move immediately puts temperance into the category of technical expertise which produces some product. Although Critias will object to Socrates treating temperance as a productive kind of expertise

(165d-166c), the meaning of self-knowledge which Critias originally associated with the Delphic maxim has been ignored.

Other times, however, Socrates does make it clear what he means by a term or what his use of a term or phrase implies, and his meaning is quite different from how the interlocutor might understand him. In such cases, Socrates takes a familiar term or phrase, shows that he is aware of its ordinary usage, and then rejects that usage explicitly. In his diatribe on rhetoric, Socrates bluntly states, 'I refuse to give the name of art to anything that is irrational' (*alogon*, 465a9). In a long segment of the *Protagoras*, Socrates redescribes moral weakness (*akrasia*) as ignorance (354e-356c). In the *Apology*, he refers to himself as a 'clever speaker' only if this means one who speaks the truth (17b3-4). There are two conflicting uses of the important term 'teaching' (*didaskein*) which prevail in Socratic discussions: 'teaching' in the sense of 'filling a passive mind with information' or 'transmitting facts from one person to another', and 'teaching', in the sense in which Socrates himself engages with others in question and answer method. Though his accusers take him to be teaching the youth not to believe in the gods of the city (*Ap.* 26b-c), Socrates is able to deny that he teaches at all, 'I was never anyone's teacher' (*Ap.* 33b-c; cf. 19d8-10).[11] In the *Meno*, learning is demonstrated to be a process of recollecting what one already knows, and 'teaching' is the bringing forth of such latent knowledge from others. Socrates draws out the right answers from the slave boy, and tells Meno to observe, 'while I merely ask questions and do not teach him' (84d1-2; cf. 85d3-4). Yet, after the demonstration is over, the ordinary use of the term 'teaching' is resumed in the dialectic. There are several key references and dramatic instances of language misuse and correction in the *Phaedo* (82b, 99b1-2, 107c, 115e5-10). Socrates' attitude with regard to the clarification of terms depends upon the dramatic context, philosophical themes, the interlocutors, or any combination of factors, but usually his dialectical approach to language is revisionist.

In cases where Socrates does persist in getting clear on what the interlocutor means by a term, his efforts may be contrasted with the eristic brothers, in the *Euthydemus*. When Euthydemus tries to refute Socrates and asks him, 'have you knowledge of something, or not?', Socrates replies that he has. When Euthydemus asks, 'do you know with that whereby you have knowledge, or with something else?' and Socrates ponders the question, saying 'I think you mean the soul, or is not that your meaning?', Euthydemus simply replies that Socrates must have some idea of what he means and tells Socrates to answer in accordance with that idea. Socrates then makes the following point: 'If you ask a question with a different meaning in your mind from that which I conceive, and I answer to the latter, are you content

I should answer nothing to the point?' (295b-d). Euthydemus says that this is acceptable to him though it is not acceptable to Socrates.

Two Examples from the Texts

Cleinias and the Eristic Brothers

The classic example of equivocation occurs early on in the *Euthydemus* when the brothers refute Cleinias with the *manthanein* equivocation (275d-276d).[12] A condensed version of their argument goes as follows:

1 Those who know, learn (e.g. 'to understand').
2 Those who do not know, learn (e.g. 'to acquire knowledge').
3 So, both those who know (the wise), and those who do not know (the ignorant), learn.

The trick and solution to the argument is contained entirely within the recognition that the term 'learn' can mean either one of two things, and in each respective sense, it applies to the wise and to the ignorant. Once the senses are disambiguated, there is no contradiction in claiming that both the wise and the ignorant learn. Unless the senses are disambiguated, however, the conclusion seems impossible as long as the wise and the ignorant are understood as opposite and mutually exclusive groups. Cleinias appears to contradict himself every time he resorts to saying the wise or the ignorant are the ones who learn, but the refutation is only apparent because he fails to distinguish between the meanings.

It is part of the comic drama of the situation that we hear Socrates as narrator speaking to Crito, explaining how much of an uproar there was from the audience of admirers watching the two brothers' performance; 'while we on our side were dismayed and held our peace' (276d3-4). Now a second bout of equivocation comes at Cleinias on the term 'know' from Euthydemus, who 'like a skillful dancer, gave a twofold twist to his questions on the same point', asking: 'do the learners learn what they know ... or what they do not?' After Cleinias is refuted again, Socrates tells him about the importance of the 'correct use of names', as Prodicus would call it, and explains the strategy that the brothers used when Cleinias gave his answers; 'how the same word is used for people who are in the opposite conditions of knowing and not knowing' (278a7-8). There is so much laughter, ridicule and play in this scene that when Socrates offers to give his version of a protreptic refutation which may fall short, he feels compelled to ask the brothers to 'restrain' themselves and 'listen without laughing' (278e5).

In his discussion of the text, Francisco Gonzalez makes a helpful remark about what Socrates does in this scene. He argues that Socrates does not fault the brothers 'for failing to clarify their terms' because it is not easy to point to one exact meaning for terms such as 'learn' or 'know'.[13] Rather, Socrates' attitude has to do with the fact that the boy has not gained anything from the experience; he would not be any 'whit the wiser as to the true state of the matters in hand' (*ta men pragmata ouden an mallon eidein pē echei*, 278b5–6). Gonzalez recognizes that the way that the brothers have conducted the refutations precludes any 'reflection' or 'insight' about the ambiguity of such terms or into the truth regarding these issues. He makes the point as follows:

> Even if the notions such as 'learning' and 'wisdom' are inherently ambiguous, there may still be a serious way of dealing with the ambiguities that illuminate these notions. The eristic method, however, is not characterized by such seriousness. It is incapable of taking seriously the only thing which the Socratic method seems to think is worth taking seriously, namely, truth.[14]

The problems with understanding Socrates' attitude towards double meaning and its dialectical appropriateness do not end here, they just begin. Socrates is about to give his first protreptic argument, and what one finds is that there are some serious complications in how he uses terminology in leading Cleinias to desire the philosophical life (278e-282d). Gonzalez closely examines this passage and identifies four fallacies in Socrates' argument.[15] I will not cover this same material, but it will help to point to a fairly standard problem with the very first line: 'Do all we human beings wish to prosper?' (*eu prattein*, 278e3).

This phrase '*eu prattein*' is used ambiguously fairly often in the dialogues; it can either mean (i) to do well, as in to 'do well at something', for example to succeed (active sense), or (ii) to fare well or prosper, as in to 'be happy' (passive sense). In the first protreptic, Socrates makes use of the double meaning by starting with (ii), moving to (i) during the argument, and concluding with (ii) 'Since we are all eager to be happy ...' (282a1). At one point, Socrates puts the question to Cleinias, 'Consider it this way: would he not err less if he did less; and so, erring less, do less ill; and hence, doing less ill be less miserable?' (281b10-c2). At *Gorgias* 507c3-5, Socrates concludes that 'the good man does well and fairly whatever he does; and that he who does well is blessed and happy'.[16] At *Charmides* 172a2-4, Socrates says 'for with error abolished, and rightness leading, in their every action men would be bound to do honorably and well under such conditions, and those who did well would be happy'.[17]

It is worth observing what R. S. W. Hawtrey has to say about the use of '*eu prattein*' in his commentary on the *Euthydemus*.[18] Hawtrey attempts to disambiguate the phrase in order to show why it is not being used ambiguously. He says:

> The ambiguity of '$εὖ πράττειν$ is apparently exploited by Plato elsewhere (e.g. *Rep.* 621d2), but not here, if the passage is correctly read, which is perhaps significant after the equivocations of the sophists. When at 279c7 $εὐτυχία$ comes into the reckoning, the emphasis shifts from in its intransitive sense (=prosper), to the sense of 'act competently', which presupposes $ἐπιστήμη$. In the intellectualist scheme of Socrates and Plato, moral behavior is normally discussed with the help of the analogy of $τέχναι$. Correct behavior can therefore be assimilated to 'competent action' and depends on knowledge; and since happiness depends in turn on correct moral behavior, there is no ambiguity in $εὖ πράττειν$.[19]

There may be no ambiguity in Socrates' interpretation, but this is not to say that there is no *use* of ambiguity, or that no ambiguity exists between Socrates' and Cleinias' understanding of the term. In a sense, there is no ambiguity for Cleinias either. He agrees that we all want to do well, on a conventional interpretation of what 'doing well' means. In my view, it is an essential part of the protreptic function that the conceptual connections, which Hawtrey notes, are eventually conveyed to Cleinias.[20] I think that what helps to convey these connections is the ambiguous use of a phrase like '*eu prattein*'. Compare the foregoing with Hawtrey's subsequent note at 282a1:

> In fact Socrates' initial question (278e3) . . . was conveniently ambiguous. The present substitution of the concept of $εὐδαιμονία$ picks up the 'prosperity' sense of $εὖ πράττειν$, while the 'efficiency' sense was exploited in the proof of the necessity for expert knowledge. It should be stressed once more that the ambiguity is of no importance for the Socratic/Platonic view of ethics, in which the two meanings coincide.[21]

The most conspicuous case for the Socratic reading of the ambiguity of '*eu prattein*' occurs in the *Protagoras*, when Socrates is misinterpreting a part of Simonides' poem that says 'If he hath fared well, every man is good; Bad, if ill' (344e7–8). Taking the context of the rest of the poem into consideration, Simonides is expressing the common opinion that it is much easier for a man who has good fortune, for whom things are going well, to be a good man than it is for he who has nothing but trouble come his way. So the phrase 'faring well' connotes 'having good luck' or 'prosperity'. Socrates turns the phrase to mean 'being good at something', and asks, as he typically does, about crafts. What is it to fare well at letters? – the study of letters. And what is it to fare well as a good doctor? – the study of medicine. So to 'fare badly' can be nothing else but the lack of knowledge. This unlikely reading of the passage helps Socrates to render the rest of the poem in a way that suits his interpretation, and has only a remote similarity to what Simonides meant or what his poem was attempting to convey. Hawtrey's point can be applied again here: the similarity between the active and passive senses of '*eu prattein*' is not remote, in Socrates' view, but closely related. His ambiguous use of the phrase enables him to put forward the interpretation which he thinks is best.

Protagoras and Folly

There is a clear case wherein Socrates plays upon the double meaning of a word for the purpose of refutation. In the *Protagoras*, Socrates tries to corner Protagoras into an agreement that all the virtues are unified as one virtue rather than split up into many parts, which is the position Protagoras has taken so far in the dialectic (332a-333b). In this case, Socrates gets Protagoras to agree immediately that folly (*aphrosunē*) is opposed to wisdom (*sophia*), where 'folly' is understood implicitly to have the sense of 'ignorance' (*amathia*). Next, Socrates argues at length that folly, understood explicitly to have the sense of 'foolishness', is opposed to temperance; he belabors the point that what is done foolishly is due to folly and the opposite of what is done temperately which is due to temperance. Then, Protagoras accepts the principle: for each thing that has an opposite, that thing has only one opposite. Based on this principle, Socrates purports to show that since Protagoras has agreed that 'folly' is the opposite of wisdom and temperance, he must now agree that wisdom and temperance are the same. This conclusion supposedly refutes Protagoras who maintains that the virtues are distinct from each other. Once the argument is formalized, and the meanings are disambiguated, it becomes obvious that an equivocation is being used.

1 Folly (in the sense of 'ignorance') is the opposite of wisdom.
2 Folly (in the sense of 'foolishness') is the opposite of temperance.
3 Each thing that has an opposite has only one opposite.
4 Therefore, wisdom and temperance are the same.

The use of the word 'folly' to mean either 'ignorance' or 'foolishness' may be acceptable in certain contexts, and given those contexts, each of the first two premises could be true, similar to the *manthanein* equivocation discussed earlier. Under the pressure of the situation and the juggling of meanings, Protagoras seems not to realize that either the third premise is being violated by the double meaning of 'folly', or that the principle which this premise signifies does not apply to words because words admit of many senses, and may have more than one opposite.[22] In either case, it is apparent that once the ambiguous use of 'folly' is cleared up, the refutation would not succeed, nor would Socrates appear to have shown the identity between wisdom and temperance. The mere observation that people use the term 'folly' in various contexts to mean either 'ignorance' or 'foolishness' does nothing to show that wisdom and temperance are, in fact, the same virtue. Unlike the eristic brothers, however, Socrates does invite Protagoras to decide which of the two incompatible statements he prefers to give up, (3) or (4), so that he may escape the problem. Protagoras cannot see how (3) can be false or rendered inapplicable to words, so he admits (4) begrudgingly (*Prt.* 333a-b).

With just a few examples, it is possible to see that for Socrates to put the tactic of ambiguity into practice, there must be an opportunity for two related but different meanings for the same expression to occur, which when manipulated or left unclarified can cause a serious misunderstanding between what the interlocutor thinks he means by what he says, and what Socrates takes him to mean. This general tactic relies on the way a term is used and when such usage produces a double meaning, there is a case of verbal ambiguity. When an ambiguous term occurs in an argument so as to make the argument invalid, a fallacy of equivocation occurs. Another tactic which affects the interlocutor's intended meaning is called '*secundum quid*', which is to take absolutely what the interlocutor meant to say only in a qualified sense by dropping a qualifying phrase from an expression.

In addition to the dialectical devices of (i) verbal ambiguity, (ii) fallacy of equivocation and (iii) *secundum quid*, there are (iv) two tactical shifts in context which cause a double meaning. One context-shift occurs between moral and non-moral, or functional, contexts. This results from Socrates' use of the techne-analogy which relies upon habitual associations made in the Greek language between the concepts of function (*ergon*), excellence or virtue (*aretē*) and art/craft (*technē*). A second context-shift has to do with a switch between an external or behavioral meaning of a term which carries a moral sense for the interlocutor, to a dispositional meaning which connotes 'power' or 'ability' and is morally neutral. However, dispositional terms will carry a moral meaning for Socrates because of the strong conceptual associations they have with cognitive or psychological states, which are understood entirely from within the context of the soul that is the source of value. Another way that Socrates alters meaning is by (v) reformulation. Frequently, Socrates reformulates what he takes the interlocutor to mean in a slightly different way than the interlocutor clearly intends it, yet the interlocutor agrees with the reformulation, seemingly unaware of any conceptual difference (*Grg.* 452e-453b; *Prt.* 319a-b; *Eu.* 14b-c).

In some instances, it is possible to track when a term or phrase which has been given a definite meaning by the interlocutor begins to lose its original sense due to one or more of these tactics. In order to see how this happens and to provide further evidence for the claim that Socrates intentionally uses such tactics, I examine two cases at length where Socrates uses some of these tactics with the interlocutors.

Refuting and Persuading Polemarchus

Polemarchus is the son of a wealthy man, Cephalus, with whom the discussion about the nature of justice was begun. Justice and money are associated with each other when Cephalus claims that the main benefit of wealth was that it enabled him to be honest and not cheat others in business transactions. It also enabled him to pay back his debts both to men and to gods (331a-c). Cephalus believes that justice and piety consist in performing these kinds of acts. In this way, justice enables an old man to die with a clear conscience and greatly reduces his fear of what may come in the afterlife. Socrates raises a problem for this very conventional view of justice by citing a case of paying back what one owes, where it is clearly an inappropriate thing to do, that is, returning borrowed weapons to a man who has gone mad (331c-d). Nor, he adds, would it be appropriate to tell the truth to such a man. Cephalus concedes and departs to tend to a sacrifice and Polemarchus takes over.

Before going any further with the refutation that takes place in four separate stages, some historical and political background will help connect the interlocutors, Cephalus and Polemarchus, to their real life counterparts. Cephalus and his family were resident aliens (*metics*) living in Athens, near the Piraeus, the port district where Socrates, in the drama, had gone down to watch the festival of Bendis. Cephalus and Polemarchus were active in the shield-making business, producing weaponry for the Athenians. The pro-democratic Athenians were fighting the Spartans and their oligarchic sympathizers in the ugly, prolonged Peloponnesian War. In effect, Cephalus and Polemarchus were earning big profits churning out weapons to give to their madmen friends, the Athenians, whom Plato perceived as men who had lost their senses and gone to war for imperialistic reasons. Once the Athenians had lost the war and were taken over by the Thirty Tyrants, Polemarchus was executed. Mark Gifford presents the idea that Plato deliberately creates tragic irony with this dramatic scenario.[23] Readers are prompted to understand the connections between the drama and the real life consequences of Polemarchus' involvement in the war. By Polemarchus' own lights, his death at the hands of his enemies corresponds to his conventional thinking about the meaning of justice.

Preliminaries

After Cephalus departs, Polemarchus, the son who will inherit everything, offers a suggestion about what it is to pay back what one owes. He cites the poet, Simonides, who said that justice is rendering to each his due (331e4-5). Polemarchus interprets this to mean that 'friends owe it to friends to do them some good and no evil' (332a9-10). In light of this, Socrates sees an important connection: a just man would not return what he borrowed, if doing so would be harmful and the person was his friend. This makes sense to Polemarchus; his formulation of Simonides' view has provided an answer to Socrates' objection to Cephalus.

Socrates notes that what is due also applies to enemies and Polemarchus agrees that enemies are owed 'some evil'. In accordance with Socrates' examples of the doctor who renders medicine to the sick, and the cook who renders flavor to food, Socrates asks what the art of justice (*techne dikaiosune*) renders and to whom. Polemarchus says, 'If we are to follow the previous examples, Socrates, it is that which renders benefits and harms to friends and enemies' (332d3-6). Socrates responds by asking, 'To do good to friends and evil to enemies, then, is justice in his meaning?' Polemarchus replies, 'I think so' (332d7-10).

The refutation of this definition contains four arguments in roughly four stages. These arguments are: (i) justice is the skill of guarding valuable things which are out of use, so justice is useless (332a-333e); (ii) the just man who is best at guarding money is also best at stealing it, hence the just man is (or has the capacity to be) a kind of thief (333e-334b); (iii) it is possible for the just man (who is supposed to be an expert at a skill) to be mistaken about his friends and enemies such that his friends are bad and his enemies are good, so accordingly justice is to help the bad and harm the good (334c-335b); and (iv) for the just man to harm his enemies means that he will make his enemies worse with respect to justice (as the moral state of a man's soul), but justice (as a *techne*) can never produce injustice (as the immoral state of a man's soul), so the just man cannot act by means of his *techne* to harm anyone (335b-e).

The First Two Stages

The first two stages of the refutation draw out the implications of treating justice as a skill since if one is to succeed at benefiting one's friends, one must know how to achieve this, and likewise with harming one's enemies. Polemarchus subscribes to a conventional idea of justice, as it is passed on to him from his father, which amounts to the rules of conduct about how to act justly in matters of war and business dealings. His idea of friendship is a mutual exchange of goods and services; a matter of utility. Expanding on this framework of skills in business, Socrates makes use of the idea of justice as an exchange, similar to the way that he handled Euthyphro's conventional idea of piety as a trading between gods and men.[24]

Socrates cites various ways in which special skills would be of service to friends with each skill having its own field of expertise. It turns out that justice has no specific field and Polemarchus gets tangled up in the paradox that justice is useful only for valuables out of use. The second refutation follows up on the concept of justice as a *technē* which implies that any skilled knowledge may be used for either good or bad ends. So, justice is not only a trivial thing, in use only when money and other valuables are out of use; the just man may now be considered a skillful thief (334a5). The remark is both outrageous and subtle, as Plato makes reference to Homer's 'complacency' (*agapa*) in portraying Odysseus' uncle Autolycus who was a gifted man in 'thievery and perjury' (334b1); one should note the same term is used earlier by Cephalus to describe himself as 'content' (330b7; with Socrates repeating the term at c5). The comparison of contexts is quite telling; Polemarchus and his father are practically being called experts in thievery in sharp ironic contrast to their view of themselves as just.

Polemarchus has no clue about how he has arrived at these paradoxes by his agreements. After these two stages, he reveals his confusion about the area of specialization with which justice is concerned, but he sticks to his definition none the less. He tells Socrates, 'I no longer know what I did mean. Yet this I still believe, that justice benefits friends and harms enemies' (334b8-10). Socrates proceeds to show him, in the terminology of friends and enemies, that the subject matter of justice is good and bad (or is it right and wrong?). It is going to make a huge difference which reading one takes of good/bad; the functional reading will exclude the notions of right/wrong, and the moral reading will include these notions. Socrates trades on both readings in order to refute and persuade Polemarchus.

Brief Analysis of the Third Stage: 334c-335b

In the third stage of the refutation, Socrates questions the meaning of 'friends' and 'enemies'. Polemarchus acknowledges the general truth that a man befriends those who seem worthy and good to him and shuns those whom he believes are not. Socrates shows him that the possibility of error about the goodness of one's friends and the badness of one's enemies affects the kind of conduct owed to each. For it may turn out that the just man who does not know who his friends and enemies are truly acts against his own advantage, and does injustice by harming the good and helping the bad. Polemarchus realizes that his original definition is flawed when he sees that it conflicts with his intuition that it is not just to harm those who have done no injustice (334d3-4). Socrates reminds him that if the just man is mistaken about his friends and enemies, then justice would be the opposite of what Simonides meant, and it would be just to harm one's friends and help one's enemies (334e1-3). Polemarchus qualifies the meaning of 'friends' and 'enemies' and decides that the friend *is* the good man and the enemy *is* the bad man (335a-b).

The Issue of Ambiguity in the Fourth Stage (335b-e)

In dealing with this stage, the results of the first three stages must be kept in mind. Polemarchus now gives two responses that set up the modified thesis that he will hold. Socrates asks whether it is the 'role' or 'part' of a just man to harm anyone (*dikaiou andros blaptein kai ontinoun anthrōpōn*, 335b3-4). Polemarchus says it is and gives his answer clearly, 'a man ought to harm (*dei blaptein*) those who are both bad and his enemies'. Polemarchus has given a moral sense to the terms 'justice' and 'harm'. The thesis which Socrates needs to refute is a conventionally moral thesis about the reciprocity of justice and it is endoxical: a just or good man returns harm for harm; not to do so is a sign of weakness and is shameful. So, it is perfectly natural to take a moral reading of Polemarchus' thesis as (P): a just man ought to harm his enemies.

A glitch occurs, however, with the meaning of 'part of' or the 'role of' a just man. One could say it is 'part of' a just man's duty and take this to mean that (i) 'it is among the things that a just man does' to harm his enemies. Or, one could say that (ii) 'it is the function of a just man' to harm his enemies. The second meaning carries the sense that returning harm for harm constitutes *in an essential way* what it means for a man to be just. Given that it is Socrates who asks the question, which meaning is more likely? I bet it is (ii). The functional or essential meaning of justice underpins the moral meaning of Polemarchus' thesis. Socrates' interpretation of Polemarchus' thesis allows the thesis to be read in two closely related but distinct ways:

(P): a just man ought to harm his enemies (moral reading).
(PP): it is the function of a just man to harm his enemies (functional reading).

Polemarchus may have intended (P), but his agreements to the analogies and premises which rest on these analogies will commit him to (PP). The readings do not conflict in the Socratic view of justice and harm; they do conflict in the conventional view.

There are, of course, a number of interpretations of this stage which scholars have put forward. Some argue that Socrates trades on a double meaning of 'harm' (*blaptein*) and attempt to specify what these meanings are: a stronger meaning is 'to make one worse', and a weaker meaning is 'to hurt' or 'cause damage to'.[25] Some have focused their attention on the techne-analogy for reasons that are related to a doctrinal analysis of Plato's views and the rest of the *Republic*. My concern is with Socrates' use of ambiguity, the protreptic function, and how the dramatic context plays into the refutation; I am not concerned with any doctrinal analysis of Plato's views in the *Republic*.

I agree with the scholars who recognize that the refutation builds implicitly on a double meaning of 'harm' (*blaptein*), for example 'to make one worse' in the Socratic sense is different from the sense that Polemarchus accepts. However, the elenctic argument that Socrates constructs is dialectical and context bound. It cannot simply be identified as equivocal in any straightforward sense, that is to say, one cannot simply disambiguate the meaning of '*blaptein*', and show that the refutation succeeds or fails on this basis alone.

It is clear that what Socrates means by 'harm' is 'what is worse with respect to the soul' and that what Polemarchus means by 'harm' is 'what is worse with respect to one's physical, social, or financial well-being'.[26] So, they both would agree, in a general way, that to harm one's enemies is to make them worse in some respect. A specific qualification is in order with regard to the Socratic meaning of harm since Socrates believes that an agent who does injustice to another person harms himself most of all. The contrast between the Socratic view of harm and the conventional view is part of the dramatic context and is one of the major themes that Plato explores in the *Republic*.

Polemarchus believes that the just man makes his enemy worse by bringing him to court, getting him incarcerated, causing him to lose money, property and honor, or by inflicting bodily harm. By contrast, Socrates does not consider such damages to be truly harmful, for as long as a man does not do injustice, nothing can harm him, not even the so-called wrongs done to him by other men (cf. *Ap.* 30c-e, 41d; *Cr.* 44c-d, 49a-d). In my account, Socrates wishes to persuade Polemarchus and not merely to refute him; so Socrates must use his own commitments and reason it out with him. Socrates' use of ambiguity is part of this process. By looking at the passage more closely, it is possible to understand how the shift to the Socratic conclusion that it is never just to harm anyone takes place (335e6-7).

The Fourth Stage of the Refutation

I have suggested two ways to read Polemarchus' thesis: (P) a just man ought to harm his enemies; and (PP) it is the function of a just man to harm his enemies. Since I believe Polemarchus intends (P), I will discuss the refutation on this moral reading, and return to the implications of the two readings in the next section. Socrates uses three analogies which help to swing the argument from a moral reading of justice and harm to a functional reading, and then back again to a moral reading. This is a persuasive strategy.

Step one. The first analogy is an animal analogy (335b3-9). To harm a horse makes it a worse horse, with respect to its virtue; to harm a dog makes it a worse dog, with respect to its virtue; and likewise to harm a man makes him a worse man, with respect to his virtue. Obviously, the pivotal term is virtue (*aretē*), which carries the implicit notion of a thing's function with it.[27] This analogy allows Socrates to establish the principle (a) to harm a thing is to make it worse with respect to its virtue; that by which horses, dogs and men are good in a functional sense. It also establishes that (b) justice is the specific virtue of man (335c4).

With this sense of goodness and justice brought in, an important qualification is dropped. In the present context, Polemarchus is talking about the just man harming those who are his enemies and who are bad. Yet, Socrates' analogy proceeds as if they were talking about harming any animal or man, bad or good. This is an example of *secundum quid*. Instead of taking the concept of harm in a qualified sense as Polemarchus intended it, to mean 'harming those who are bad', Socrates proceeds as if Polemarchus had meant 'harming anyone'. But Polemarchus has already agreed that it is not just to harm those who are good; the analogy seems to neutralize any moral sense of the terms at this point. Socrates uses the animal analogy presumably with the idea in mind that to harm those who are bad makes them more unjust than they already are. This may be true, in Socratic terms, but it does not address Polemarchus' point. Polemarchus' idea from the start is that to harm the unjust is a form of retaliation or punishment, which is not a way of making them more unjust, but more just! In the conventional view, punitive retaliation is a form of social justice; it brings restitution and provides a corrective. Protagoras takes this conventional perspective with an emphasis on its rationality in his Great Speech (*Prt.* 324a-326e), and Socrates discusses his version of this type of justice with Polus (*Grg.* 477a-e).

Nevertheless, in agreeing with the terms of the analogy, Polemarchus must agree with conclusion (c).

(a)   to harm a man is to make him worse with respect to his virtue (335b9-c2).
(b)   justice is the specific virtue of humans (335c3-4).
(c)   to harm a man makes him more unjust (335c6).

Step two. Socrates uses a second analogy of the just man as expert to the musical expert who cannot, by his knowledge, make another unmusical, and the horse trainer who cannot, by his knowledge, make other men unfit for horse training. Polemarchus agrees. Socrates caps it off with a third analogy that puts an emphasis on natural forces and their functions. It is not the function (*ergon*) of heat nor of dryness to produce their opposites (335d2-4). Socrates takes the notion of function, and implicitly − by a slide − he applies it to that 'of the good' (*tou agathou*).[28] Now he asks whether the just man is good. Polemarchus agrees and this brings the argument back to justice as a moral quality. On the basis of the two strategies of argument by analogy, Socrates establishes that

(d)   the just man, by justice, can never produce injustice (335d2-4),

and concludes that:

(e)   it is not the function (*ergon*) of the just man to harm anyone (335e6-7).

By means of the three analogies: an animal analogy, a techne-analogy and a natural forces analogy, Socrates has changed Polemarchus' conventionally moral concepts of harm and justice to a Socratic sense, and he has done this without a blatant equivocation on the meaning of the terms. He has moved from the external to the internal senses of these concepts by relying upon the closely related but ambiguous notions of moral and functional goodness. Before the analogies, the benefits and harms which the various professional skills render belonged to the external and non-moral domains of war, finance, cooking, farming, sailing across the sea and medicine for the body (332c-333e). After the analogies, it appears that the only harm the just man can do to his enemies who are bad is an internal harm, in particular, an unjust harm. This implies that justice belongs essentially to the character of a man, and, in particular, to the man's soul rather than to his actions or to his social or financial status. Once the concepts of harm and justice are internalized, the just man who has the knowledge to benefit the good and harm the bad cannot possibly use his knowledge to harm another. The just man is no longer the expert, referred to in the second stage, as one who can use his knowledge for good or bad ends. Also by means of the analogy to musical experts and to natural forces, Socrates establishes the connection between virtue as a state or power of the soul and the kind of conduct that must result from it.[29] These analogies allow Socrates to refute Polemarchus' definition of justice, and at the same time, Polemarchus' conventional position has been given a thoroughly Socratic interpretation by means of them.

Objections

The drama shows that Socrates has been successful in refuting Polemarchus. He says, 'it has been made clear to us that in no case is it just to harm anyone' (335e6-7), and Polemarchus agrees to take a stand on Socrates' side against those who think otherwise. The use of ambiguity is a dialectical strategy that capitalizes on the close relationship that already exists between the moral and non-moral or prudential contexts, as reflected in the terminology of 'function', 'virtue', 'good' and 'beneficial'. The use of ambiguity is integral to SM because Socrates' moral position is grounded in the view that a compatible link exists between moral and prudential domains. This link is supported by Socrates' revisionist strategy.

A likely objection to my interpretation is that I have assumed too strong a distinction between the moral reading (P) and functional reading (PP) of Polemarchus' thesis and treated them as exclusive when they really belong together. Polemarchus does not make such a sharp distinction between the moral and functional contexts. If the difference between contexts is not so sharp, then the shifts in context would not be the important source of ambiguity that I claim it to be. If Polemarchus holds a moral/functional thesis of justice and accepts the techne-analogy, then his view of justice stays intact at least through step one, and no ambiguity is involved.

I will use (PP) and run through the argument again briefly. Given his agreement (c) to harm a man makes him more unjust, Polemarchus is committed to the claim that the just expert in harming his enemies, and making them more unjust, makes them less able to help their friends and harm their enemies. This is acceptable on his account; for the just man to harm his enemies by incapacitating them in this way makes perfect sense. In step two, however, Polemarchus loses out. By agreeing that the just expert can never produce injustice, he is accepting the opposite situation which is unfavorable given his view of justice. If the just expert can never, by the exercise of justice, make anyone less just, then the only alternative for Polemarchus' meaning of justice is that the just expert would make his enemies more able to help his friends and harm his enemies. And this outcome refutes Polemarchus' position on his own view of justice.[30]

Granted, in step one, both Socrates and Polemarchus on their own views of justice would agree with the premises. But the point is that they would be agreeing for different reasons, though it is true that Polemarchus' view is not yet undermined. What step two shows, however, is that while the moral and functional contexts are closely related to each other for Socrates and Polemarchus, the way that the two contexts are related is very different. I can allow for the moral-functional reading of Polemarchus' thesis and agree that the moral and non-moral contexts are closely related in the Greek way of thinking.

I agree that the difference in meaning between moral and non-moral contexts is not very wide nor is it sharply delineated, but the fact that the moral and non-moral contexts are closely related makes it more difficult for the interlocutor to distinguish between meanings rather than less difficult. Just because the terms are used in contexts that are closely related does not mean that they are not used ambiguously, especially if the interlocutor takes the meaning in one way and Socrates takes it in another way. Thus, the objection that the moral and non-moral contexts are closely related does not affect my thesis negatively.

The reason why I call Socrates' use of ambiguity a dialectical strategy is that such terms remain ambiguous until the moral or prudential context is determined, and this ambiguity allows Socrates to switch back and forth between the contexts, in a deliberate manner, to suit the needs of the refutation. He shifts contexts as if it makes no difference which sense of a term is being used. But it does make a difference. The interlocutor agrees to premises only because he takes Socrates to be referring to the meaning of a term as he, the interlocutor, interprets it. If he takes the meaning of a term, in a moral sense, and Socrates uses the term as if the interlocutor took it in a non-moral sense, or vice-versa, then Socrates is using ambiguity in the way that I claim him to be.

If one objects that there is no deliberate use of ambiguity because Socrates sincerely believes in the connection between moral and prudential domains, I would agree that this is true. There may be no ambiguity for Socrates because on his interpretation the terminology is consistent and univocal. But if one argues that not only does Socrates sincerely believe that there is a connection made between moral and functional excellence, but so do the interlocutors, I would not agree. While there is some sense in which the interlocutor believes in a connection between the moral and non-moral domains, I argue that the interlocutor only appears to follow Socrates' meaning. I think that the fact that the interlocutor is refuted by his own agreement to the premises supports my position.

Polemarchus is a non-sophistic interlocutor, in Group 2, who said what he sincerely believes. He tries to defend a conventional view of justice and fails. He does not have a problem with admitting that he was refuted and changing over to Socrates' side. Because of the ambiguities involved in the refutation, the argument that Socrates puts forth against Polemarchus' conventional view of justice is invalid, strictly speaking. Yet, Polemarchus seems genuinely convinced. In my view, this is because Polemarchus has shown himself to be more committed to the belief that harming those who are good and just, even unintentionally, is unjust and something to be avoided. This realization helps to change his belief in his original definition of justice, at least to the extent that he has seen that knowledge has a role to play in the concept of justice. And I would like to add that this is the case even if the reasoning that Socrates uses to refute Polemarchus is formally invalid. Socrates has had a positive influence on Polemarchus' thinking, and this is what matters for Socrates and his moral aim to improve the interlocutor.

Polus and the Desire for Power

In the *Gorgias*, there is an extended conversation between Socrates and Polus and a series of refutations which is typically divided into three (467c-468e; 474b-475c; 476a-480a). I am concerned with the first refutation which takes place in two stages. The first stage sets up the terminology that will support the distinction between 'doing what one wants' and 'doing what seems best' (466b-467c). The second stage begins with Polus' staunch rejection of this distinction as implausible and culminates in something just short of a verbal admission to the opposite of his original thesis (467c-468e). To limit my discussion, I must bypass the opening segment between Socrates and Polus which takes place just after Gorgias has been refuted (461b-466a).

Analysis of the First Stage: 466b-467c

Socrates ends his lengthy account of rhetoric with a self-conscious remark that he has just given a long speech after asking Polus to be brief (465e). He justifies the behavior by claiming that Polus was not able to understand him when he answered briefly and apparently could not 'make any use' (*oude chrēsthai*) of the answers. Now that the speech is finished, Socrates challenges him again, 'if you can make any use of this answer of mine, do so' (466a4). Polus did not comprehend much of what Socrates has said, so he repeats what he takes to be Socrates' claim that rhetoric is flattery. Socrates corrects him with the phrase a 'branch of flattery'. Polus wonders whether Socrates would extend his claim to good orators (*hoi agathoi rhētores*), and he asks if Socrates really thinks they are considered worthless in their own cities. Socrates answers that 'they are not considered at all' (466b4). This blunt response brings Polus and Socrates to the main issue of whether orators have 'great power' (*megiston dunatai*) in the cities. In the next few lines, Polus tries to strengthen his position by appealing to tyrants as the perfect example of what it is to have great power in the city.

The difference of opinion between Socrates and Polus must be stated clearly since the refutation is a confusing piece of argument. Socrates says that orators and tyrants have 'the least power in their cities'. He thinks this because 'they do nothing they wish to do', although, as Socrates admits, 'they do whatever they think is best' (*Grg.* 466d-e). Polus says the opposite: orators and tyrants have great power in their cities. However, Socrates insists that Polus cannot really hold to his claim since Polus has agreed that 'great power is a good to him who has it' (466e6-7).

In this scene, Polus continues to be the questioner and Socrates the answerer. Socrates and Polus agree to premise (1): great power is a good thing for the man who has it (466e7, 467a4, 468e2). The concept of power is associated, in Polus' mind, with the possession of something good, as a means, on the understanding that having such power enables the agent to do or to get whatever he wants. Polus is trying to defend his view that orators are valued in the city because, as Gorgias had claimed earlier (452d-e), they have great political power and rule over others; this power is similar to the power that a tyrant has over the life and death of those he controls.

The pace is quickened because Socrates starts asking questions out of turn. He presses Polus to agree that (2) those who lack intelligence make mistakes about what is best for themselves, and (3) doing what one wants is not the same as doing what seems best, without intelligence. Socrates does not have much trouble getting Polus' agreement to (1) and (2), but he will have difficulty getting Polus to agree with (3). In this section, I examine premises (1) and (2) both from the standpoint of Polus and from the Socratic standpoint, in order to show how Socrates eventually derives his position that orators and tyrants are powerless in their cities from premises which Polus accepts.

Premise (1): great power is a good for the one who has it. Given Polus' idea of power and its relation to the good, the meaning of (1) conveys a non-moral context of a thing's being good, insofar as it appears good for the agent who possesses it. In this context, the concept of good refers to whatever is being pursued or aimed at by the agent, regardless of its moral value. Power represents the means to get whatever the agent wants.[31] In this way, premise (1) suggests both the 'ability' and the 'desire' for the 'apparent' good. When Polus agrees to (1), what he thinks is that great power is desirable and he assumes that whatever is desirable to the agent is good. This is quite the opposite of what Socrates takes him to mean, and gets him to commit to, which is that great power is not desirable as a good at all, unless it is used with intelligence.

Socrates does not explicitly draw out Polus' interpretation of (1) but he would consider it to be false as it stands. A Socratic interpretation of (1) could render it true. For Socrates, the concept of goodness is always grounded in knowledge, and so, if power is a good thing, it must be related to knowledge or intelligence. For instance, 'power' has this meaning when Socrates suggests the association of power or knowledge in the soul with justice to Hippias, in the *Hippias Minor* (375d8-9). In such cases where the term 'power' has a favorable meaning for Socrates, the claim that great power is a good thing would require that 'good' refers to a moral end. Clearly, Socrates would agree with Polus' interpretation of power as an ability, but this ability is knowledge, or, in the present case, having the intelligence to achieve what one desires. For Socrates, since one always desires the real good, knowledge of the good is the only thing that one needs to possess the good.

The Socratic interpretation of premise (1) lies beneath Socrates' reminders to Polus of his agreement to the truth of the premise. Exactly at the point where having power is supposed to guarantee the good for the agent, but doing what seems best may turn out to be bad for the agent (466e1-467a), Socrates focuses on the need for intelligence (*nous*, 466e7, 467a5), and from this point forward, 'intelligence' qualifies and restricts Polus' conception of power, in the same way that Socrates' interpretation of *technē* had restricted Gorgias' conception of rhetoric earlier (449c-461b).

Socrates had already made it quite clear that he thinks orators have no knowledge of what is best for their listening audience and that rhetoric is not an art. He reminds Polus of this view explicitly near the end of the first stage (467a-b). Socrates' view of the orator's lack of knowledge is equated with and transfers over to the idea of tyrants doing what seems best without intelligence, and not knowing what really is best for themselves. So, for both orators and tyrants, if they act without intelligence when they do what they think is best, they cannot do what is good for them, and hence they lack great power.

In the conversation, there are two widely different conceptions of intelligence. When Polus agrees that orators and tyrants need intelligence to gain benefit from their actions, he is not referring to the knowledge of what is just and unjust, but to what is good and bad for the agent, in a prudential sense of the terms. For Socrates, however, knowledge of what is just and unjust is simply another way to interpret knowledge of what is good and bad for the agent. Even though Polus has allowed that tyrants and orators need intelligence, his idea of intelligence is cleverness, which is clearly different from Socrates' conception of intelligence as knowledge of what is morally best.

Earlier, Socrates had directly challenged Polus either to prove that orators are intelligent or to leave Socrates unrefuted. Notice what Socrates is not asking Polus to do. Socrates is not asking him to explain what he means by 'intelligence' in an effort to become clear on how each of them conceives of the notion. What Socrates demands is to hear the counter-argument against his view from a rhetor, such as Polus, who will thereby demonstrate, through his own speech, his intelligence by arguing on behalf of his profession. The connection between the *logoi* and the characters reverberates in the drama. According to Socrates, the lack of intelligence which is openly displayed in dramatic terms by Polus automatically rules out the possibility that the orators and tyrants can do what is good for them, and if they can't do what is good for them, they have no power. Polus needs to clarify what he means by 'intelligence' for he apparently believes that a tyrant or orator could not have great power unless he is intelligent.

The original point that Polus wanted to make in claiming that orators, like tyrants, have great power in the city is that tyrants are powerful, insofar as they are successful in achieving what they set out to do, regardless of whether such action is just or unjust, and despite occasional errors in judgment. Polus' assumption is not unlike Thrasymachus' which is that the tyrant would not be a successful tyrant if he made a lot of careless errors. If the tyrant repeatedly misjudged what is in his own interest, in his political activities, he would not be a tyrant for very long. And the same goes for the rhetor, who would not exert much influence over his listeners if he was incompetent. Polus stands for the 'tried and true' methods of rhetoric but in this particular instance these methods do not come through for him for he lacks the experience in dialectic which he requires to succeed. Polus fails not only to clarify the orator's conception of intelligence, he fails to exhibit it.

Formally, up to this point, it was Polus who was supposed to be questioning Socrates, though Socrates directs the discussion, and asks Polus questions as well. At the end of the first stage (467c5), Polus claims that he is ready to answer Socrates' questions in order to understand what Socrates means by such an implausible distinction.

Analysis of the Second Stage: 467c-468e

Premises (1) and (2) put important qualifications on what Polus originally meant, and his agreements imply that power is not the kind of good that he thought it was. The two qualifications contrast sharply with the meaning of 'doing what seems best' and clearly show that premise (3) is true: to do what merely seems best, without intelligence, is not the same as doing what one wants. Socrates has agreed that orators and tyrants do what they think is best, but he has denied that this gives them great power due to the need for intelligence to achieve their good, so Socrates subsequently denies that they do what they want (467b).

Polus is agitated by what he believes to be purely a verbal distinction that Socrates has made between 'doing what one wants' and 'doing what seems best', despite the parallel distinction between 'doing what is good with intelligence', and 'doing what seems good without intelligence', which he has already accepted. Though the distinction itself seems counter-intuitive, the reasoning behind the distinction which Socrates draws out of Polus' agreement is straightforward. When we do what we think best, without intelligence, we don't always do what is good. Yet, we always want what is good, in our actions, so doing what seems best, without intelligence, and doing what one wants, cannot be the same. Polus is able to discriminate between those actions done without error which benefit one's interest and those done by mistake which do not, but he does not recognize the possibility that one may be mistaken about what one desires, nor does he realize that there is a distinction to be made between the apparent and the real good, as objects of desire. Polus has agreed to premises (1) and (2), but he gives these two premises an interpretation which allows him to think that the two expressions of premise (3) are equivalent in meaning. To get Polus to accept premise (3), Socrates works on getting him to agree with premise (4): whenever one acts, one wants to do the action only if it is good (468c5-6). This premise is a version of psychological eudaimonism.

To support the distinction in (3), Socrates directs the discussion to the ends of actions rather than to the actions themselves. In this stage, the structure of the refutation is difficult to follow, but his strategy is clear. Socrates establishes a means-ends context for action and desire. He uses two familiar kinds of non-moral actions and their aims, that is, taking medicine for the sake of health and sailing for the goal of wealth (467c-d), and generalizes to the strong eudaimonist principle of action.

> If a man does something for an object, he does not wish the thing that he does, but the thing for which he does it (467d8-10).

Next, Socrates suggests a classification that distinguishes between good things, bad things and those that are neither good nor bad, the intermediate things (467e2-468b1). Polus accepts the classification, and the claim that we do the intermediate things for the good things (468a7-10). The strong version of the eudaimonist principle of action is formulated again in four consecutive lines. With reference to the actions of a tyrant, who puts people to death, exiles them and takes their property, Socrates asks Polus, as a reminder,

> So it is for the sake of the good that the doers of all things do them? (468b5-6).

And again,

> ... we have admitted that when we do things for an object, we do not wish those things, but the object for which we do them? (468b8-10).

Polus agrees with the strong version. Yet the principle will be changed slightly, and seems to be weakened, perhaps, to allow for the point that means, such as actions, can be desired, in some sense. With regard to the tyrant's actions, Socrates says that one does not wish any of these actions in themselves, but

> ... if these things are beneficial we wish to do them, while if they are harmful, we do not wish them (468c5-6).

Socrates has turned the eudaimonist principle of action into a conditional statement which is expressed by premise (4): whenever one acts, one wants to do the action only if it is good (or beneficial).

Also, in this stage of the refutation, Socrates seems to equivocate between 'the goods' which he allows initially to be objects of desire, and 'the good' which becomes the only thing that is really beneficial, and hence is the true object of desire.[32] The equivocation begins at 467c5, where Socrates uses the examples of the conventional goods of health and wealth and treats these goods as ends. In particular, the difference in language indicates the equivocation in the passage (468a7-9), where Socrates asks Polus whether we do intermediate things (*ta metaxu*) for the sake of good things (*ta agatha*) or good things for the sake of intermediate things, and Polus answers that we do the intermediate for the good things (*ta agatha*). Then Socrates asks:

> Thus it is in pursuit of the good (*to agathon*) that we walk, when we walk, conceiving it to be better; or on the contrary, stand, when we stand, for the sake of the same thing, the good: (*tou agathou*): is it not so? Yes (468b1-4).

The inference is carried over to the actions of killing, exiling and confiscating. Whenever such actions are done, they are done because they are thought to be better. And here is where Socrates restates the strong formulation of the eudaimonist principle, using the singular phrase *tou agathou*, when he says, 'So it is for the sake of the good that the doers of all these things do them' (468b5-6).

The ambiguity in the meaning of desire is related to the change in the meaning of 'good' in the above set of passages. The ambiguity which arises is that Polus understands that the desire for what is good is determined by what the agent thinks is good, and this corresponds to his conception of the 'good things', which Socrates has just mentioned. However, Socrates has already established the condition for what the good is, through the concept of intelligence, in the first stage. In the second stage, the good will be demarcated not by what the agent thinks are the 'good things' but what is, in fact, the 'real' good. The refutation comes to an end when Socrates gets Polus to agree, again, that if a man (tyrant or orator) kills someone or confiscates a person's property, he only wants to do these actions if he thinks it is 'better' (*ameinōn*) for himself, but he does not want to do them if 'it is really worse' (*tugchanei de on kakion*) (468d1-4). Next, Socrates asks him whether he thinks that a man who does such actions, does what he thinks is best. Polus agrees (468d5-7). Then, Socrates asks Polus, 'Now is it also what he wishes, supposing it to be really bad (*kaka onta*)?' (468d8-10). Polus reluctantly admits that, in such a case, a man does not do what he wants. Polus has agreed to premise (4) that a man can desire an action, only if that action leads to the good, and since Socrates has just stated the condition, in terms of what is, in fact, good, Polus is cornered into admitting the terminological distinction he did not want to admit.

As a result of his agreement to premises (1) and (4), and due to his inability to distinguish between meanings of 'intelligence' and oppose premise (2), Polus winds up accepting premise (3) and is refuted. In order to get Polus in this position, Socrates uses dialectical strategies. He works with two different conceptions of 'intelligence', without further clarification. Due to a failure to distinguish on Polus' part, the idea that someone can make a mistake in his own interest gets connected to a lack of intelligence. Socrates sets up the means–ends context for action and gets Polus to accept the principle that everyone desires good things. Socrates equivocates between 'good things' and 'the good'; he stipulates that 'the good' be equated with the 'real' good, and not the 'good things', which are equated with the 'apparent' good.

The refutation is not closed formally because Polus does not acknowledge the truth of Socrates' conclusion that a man may do what seems best and yet not do what he wants, so the conversation continues and intensifies. Polus shifts the terms of the conversation to happiness, and asks whether Socrates would not envy a man who has the power to put people to death and send them to prison. With this question, the issue finally comes around to justice and injustice and Polus makes his indifference to the moral outcome plain when he indicates that it doesn't matter how the act is done, such a man is enviable in either case (469a1-2).

Conclusion

In this section, I offer my view of what it is that Socrates is trying to show Polus in this refutation. Socrates wants to show that Polus does not really desire power, nor does anyone else, because power is not a good, either as an end or as a means. In the first stage, Socrates points out that power is not a good as an end because power alone does not meet the criterion of success in achieving what is good. The criterion of success in achieving what is good entails that a man who has power must have intelligence. In the second stage, Socrates uses the means–end framework to show Polus that power is not a good as a means. Means are neither good nor bad, and they are never desired unconditionally. Once the desire for power is put into the category of means which can only be desired conditionally, Socrates shows that power does not meet the condition of what is actually good for the agent because it always requires intelligence to benefit its possessor. Socrates has made the same argument in both stages with slightly different formulations. In the final analysis, Socrates has tried to show that Polus cannot really desire power as end or as a means. Socrates shows Polus not only that Polus does not know what he believes, but also that he does not know what he desires.

To a greater or lesser extent, Polus agrees with the premises that bring about his refutation, but his thesis is not genuinely refuted due to ambiguity. Moreover, Socrates does not convince Polus of the conclusion nor has Socrates convinced Polus that he does not desire power as a good thing. Polus thinks that the claim that orators and tyrants have great power in the city is an empirical claim which anyone can verify as true by observation. Socrates has turned the claim into a conceptual issue with premise (3), and his insistence on the conceptual distinction. In my view, Socrates does this because he believes that in order to affect Polus' actions in his pursuit of rhetoric, he needs to change Polus' thinking about the concepts of power, intelligence, good and desire. But Polus is not persuaded. He does not cease to desire power as a good thing, nor does he stop pursuing the practice of rhetoric, just because Socrates shows him that on a certain conception of 'good' and 'desire', it is not possible for Polus to desire power. Polus does not believe that he is wrong to desire power because he thinks that everyone desires it. Polus has the support of popular opinion which, as an orator, is the only support he deems necessary. So despite his agreement to the premises of the elenctic argument, Polus shows no sign of changing his opinion of rhetoric and its power.

I have argued that the premise, great power is a good thing for the man who has it, is true, according to both Polus and Socrates, provided that the premise is understood to mean two different things. The same can be said for the meaning of the premise that justice is the specific virtue of a human being which is agreed upon by Polemarchus and Socrates. In each case, the endoxical premises may be turned into protreptic premises. If the premises are understood with the specific Socratic interpretation assigned to them, they transform into the following Socratic claims: great power is knowledge which is the only good thing; justice is the virtue that is always beneficial to the soul.

Chapter 4

Ambiguity and Drama

Introduction

Plato offers his readers a dual perspective with which to view Socratic argumentation as it plays out in the drama. The elenctic argument purportedly
relies on the interlocutor's own premises to refute his thesis. The protreptic
argument relies on these same premises in an attempt to persuade him of a
Socratic moral position. In the first case, the interlocutor's conventional
views and misunderstanding of the terms or premises have a negative effect
within the dramatic frame. The interlocutor's thesis appears to be refuted
and he is caught in a contradiction; he experiences *aporia*, or shame, or
other psychological effects. Outside the dramatic frame, at the textual
level, the reader may recognize that the argument Socrates constructs is
invalid due to the ambiguity of the terms or some other fallacy. On all
accounts, Socrates needs a set of premises which have been genuinely
agreed to be true by the interlocutor and a valid argument to refute the interlocutor's thesis. In my interpretation, Socrates' use of ambiguity prevents
any real agreement to the premises and there is no genuine refutation of the
interlocutor's thesis. However, the interlocutor himself has been refuted
since he failed to distinguish meanings and verbally agreed to the premises.

In the second case, a revised understanding of the same terms may give
way to a Socratic meaning, result in a protreptic argument and suggest a
solution to the *aporia*. Again, this scenario occurs at the dramatic level.
As an example, I have presented the refutation of Polemarchus who has taken
the side of Socrates, though I do not claim that Polemarchus was shown to be
aware of the Socratic terminology. At the textual level, the reader would
be expected to work out for himself whether the protreptic argument is valid
or sound. And then, of course, when Thrasymachus barges in, a whole other
sequence of ideas, terms and arguments takes over, at both dramatic and
textual levels.

SM is a revisionist methodology. Socrates tries to lift the interlocutor out
of his conventional patterns of thought and offers him a new set of concepts
that will enable him to think philosophically. Socrates does not have a new

set of terms to go with these concepts, so he takes liberties with the meanings of words and extends them beyond their ordinary usage. This sort of dialectical activity is what makes Socrates a remarkable dialectician and a moral reformer rather than an educator or eristic debater.

In raising the issue of the use of ambiguity in the SM, it is not my intention merely to analyse the dialectical arguments or point out the flaws in Socrates' reasoning. Nor do I wish to figure out various ways in which the interlocutor could have avoided the appearance of being refuted. Instead, I have set about examining the dialectical context to determine what purpose a given argument has in the drama and why Plato has Socrates use a particular ambiguity or fallacy in that argument with a certain interlocutor. These tasks cannot be accomplished within a purely formalist view of fallacy for this view is concerned solely with the logical status or validity and soundness of the arguments; this approach can do no more than show why Socrates succeeds or fails in his reasoning.

Socratic dialectical arguments occur in conversations which give the arguments a distinctive context. The conversation and the characters are situated in a dramatic field and there is movement to the dialogue as a whole. The arguments develop out of a set of themes and a few key terms emerge which are shown not to be clearly understood. Socrates magnifies the problem and in the process he extends the meaning of the concepts which the terms signify. There is much dramatic innuendo, however, that points towards what the argument is about, and explains why Socrates takes the particular path he does with that interlocutor. Ambiguity is central to Socratic argumentation but ambiguity has a larger role to play in the literary arts and so too in Plato's dialogues. To get a sense of the importance of language use and misuse at a more general level, I provide an overview of the concept of ambiguity.

Historical Background

Aristotle

The first critical approach to ambiguity and fallacy comes from Plato's satire of eristic method in the *Euthydemus*. The systematic approach begins with Aristotle's classification of ambiguity in conjunction with his theory of fallacy, or sophistical refutation, in the *Sophistici Elenchi*, which is appended to his work, the *Topics*, a treatise on dialectical reasoning. According to Aristotle, 'a refutation . . . is reasoning (*sullogismos*) accompanied by contradiction of the conclusion' (*SE* 165a3). A sophistical refutation is not really a refutation at all, but a fallacy (*paralogismos*); it is one that appears to be a genuine refutation, but is not (164b20-21; cf. 169b19-28).

In chapter 4, Aristotle divides the general group of fallacies into two main categories: those fallacies which depend on language and those which do not. He presents six types of fallacy that are dependent on language (165b23-24), and seven types that are not (166b20-25).[1] The six types of linguistic fallacy are homonymy (lexical ambiguity), amphiboly (syntactic ambiguity), combination of words, division of words, wrong accent and form of expression used.[2] The seven types of non-linguistic fallacy are accident, the use of words absolutely or in a certain respect, ignorance of a refutation, assumption of original point, consequent, non-cause as cause and making of two questions into one.[3] Aristotle approaches ambiguity entirely within a discussion of fallacy. Of the six types of fallacy supposedly dependent on language, homonymy and amphiboly are the two main types that are concerned with ambiguity, understood as double meaning (165b35, 166a14, 168a24-25).

In Aristotle's account, there is some confusion as to the relation between ambiguity and fallacy because the type of ambiguity is supposed to identify the fallacy, but Aristotle recognizes that not all of the fallacies that he classifies as dependent on language are produced by ambiguity, for instance, the fallacy of accent. Combination and division are classified as types of amphiboly, and so there are not really six types of ambiguity (168a24-34). At the end of his discussion on how to resolve the fallacies of combination and division of words, Aristotle says, 'Therefore an expression whose meaning turns on division is not ambiguous (*ou ditton*), and it is clear also that all refutations do not turn upon ambiguity as some people say' (*SE* 177b8-10).

In chapter 5, Aristotle develops his definition of a refutation in more detail and introduces the fallacy he describes as 'ignorance of what a refutation is' (*ignoratio elenchi*). This fallacy may be understood as one particular type among the 13 fallacies. Or, it may be taken as a general heading under which the 12 fallacy types can be grouped, as Aristotle explains in chapter 6. In chapter 5, he claims that a refutation must be a

> contradiction of one and the same predicate, not of a name but of a thing, and not of a synonymous name but of an identical name, based on the given premises [*sic*] and following necessarily from them (the original point at issue not being included) in the same respect, relation, manner and time (167a21-28).

In chapter 6, Aristotle explains how each of the 12 fallacy types falls short of the definition one way or another, and so whenever a particular refutation does not satisfy the definition of a refutation, it will be a false refutation since it fails to contradict the thesis to be refuted, though it may appear to contradict it (168a17-24; cf. 168b17-22, 169b9-13).[4]

Aristotle is concerned, in chapter 7, to connect his definition to those false refutations that depend on the linguistic fallacies, whereby the 'deception' (*apatē*) comes from the failure to distinguish meaning and this occurs especially with terms such as 'unity', 'being' and 'identity' (169a24; cf. 182b22-7). The general point to be taken from this discussion put in less technical language is this. Ignorance of the refutation occurs when the interlocutor is unaware of the meaning of what a refutation is, and so he thinks that the conclusion drawn by the questioner is the conclusion which refutes his proposed thesis, but actually it is not – some other conclusion has been drawn instead. The interlocutor is unaware of what exactly constitutes the opposite of his thesis, so he cannot recognize when his thesis has been overturned, and when it only appears to have been overturned. From this formulation, it seems to be the interlocutor's ignorance that is responsible for the fallacy. However, formulated differently, this fallacy is the generic fallacy known, in contemporary jargon, as 'irrelevant conclusion'. In this formulation, the ignorance of the interlocutor is not referred to and is not considered to be the source of the fallacy. Rather, the fallacy is due to the questioner attempting to distract the interlocutor from the conclusion in any number of ways, depending on the type of error committed.

A dialectical refutation depends on the intuitive and critical skills, and on the attitudes and dispositions, of the persons involved in the argument, on what is being argued and with whom, and in what context. Aristotle says explicitly that a 'sophistical refutation is not an absolute refutation but is relative to some person' (170a13-14), and that those who depend on equivocation refute sophistically and only appear to refute because 'they have not secured a statement which has a single meaning but only one which appears to be such, and only for a particular person' (170a16-19). What Aristotle endeavors to do, in the *Sophistici Elenchi*, is to identify and to resolve the various fallacies, by explaining why someone might be deceived into thinking he has been genuinely refuted, and how to avoid the appearance of being refuted.

As part of Aristotle's account of fallacy, he makes extensive comments on how ambiguity and other fallacious moves are used in sophistic refutations. On the need to draw distinctions between meanings, the whole of chapter 17 is relevant because Aristotle is trying to explain the need to block the appearance of being refuted by a sophistical refutation. He says:

However, since, if one does not distinguish the meanings of a doubtful term, it is not clear whether he has been confuted or not and since the right to draw distinctions is conceded in arguments, it is obvious that to grant the question simply without making distinctions is a mistake; so that, even if the man himself does not appear to be refuted, yet his argument certainly appears to be so (175b28-34).

Aristotle explains that people may even 'see the ambiguity', but they refrain from making distinctions because of the pressure of the crowd, or in order not to anger the questioner, or because they assumed the argument would not depend on such ambiguity. In sum, Aristotle says 'since the right to draw a distinction is conceded, we must not hesitate to use it, as was said before' (175b38-39).

In chapter 19, he explains how those refutations which depend on ambiguity and amphiboly work. The double meaning may be in the questioning or in the conclusion of an argument. He notes:

When the diversity of meaning occurs in the questions, there is no need to deny the ambiguity beforehand; for the argument is not directed towards it as a conclusion but carried on by means of it. At the beginning, therefore, one ought to reply to an ambiguous term or expression in the following manner, that 'in one sense it is so and in another it is not so' (177a20-25).

Throughout the *Topics*, Aristotle offers advice about how to refute and avoid being refuted due to ambiguity in the context of dialectical reasoning.[5] In Book I, he notes '[F]or if the various ways in which a term can be used are not clear, it is possible that the answerer and questioner are not applying their mind to the same thing' (108a22-25). In Book V, he says that 'one must not use as signifying properly either a word or an expression which is used with several meanings, because anything which has several meanings renders the statement obscure, since he who is about to argue is doubtful which of the various meanings his opponent is using' (129b35-130a4).

Again, in *Topics* I.18, Aristotle recognizes the need to distinguish meanings as a necessary part of one's dialectical practice. He says:

It is also useful so that one may not be misled and that one may mislead others by false reasoning. For if we know the various senses in which a term can be used, we shall never be misled by false reasoning, but we shall be aware of it if the questioner fails to direct his argument to the same point; and we shall ourselves, when we are asking questions, be able to mislead the answerer, if he does not happen to know the various meanings of a term (108a26-30).

With an important caveat which he apparently feels he must attach, Aristotle continues: 'This kind of argument, however, is not a proper part of dialectic; therefore, dialecticians must be very much on their guard against such verbal discussion, unless it is quite impossible to discuss the subject otherwise' (108a33-36).

These quotations, and there are many more, are sufficient to establish Aristotle's special concern with ambiguity and its relation to fallacy. It is worth noting that both in his discussion of dialectic, in the *Topics*, and of sophistical reasoning in the *SE*, Aristotle advises the questioner and the answerer on debating tactics. Of equal importance is Aristotle's candid advice on concealment in debating in *Topics* VIII.1 (155b26-157a5) and in the *SE* 174b14-15, and especially at 174a27-29, where he says, 'In a word, all the resources for concealment mentioned before are also useful against competitive arguments; for concealment is for the purpose of escaping detection, and escape from detection is for the purpose of deception'. While it is necessary to keep in mind that Aristotle's conception of dialectic and its aim is different from Socrates' and Plato's in important respects, it is useful to understand how liberal the conduct is between the questioner and answerer in a dialectical context, and that many of the same debating tactics are allowed in both the dialectical and the sophistic style of argumentation. In other words, they may both use the same tactics.[6]

Aristotle also mentions ambiguity in his account of rhetorical method in the *Rhetoric*. In Book III.2, he discusses style (*lexis*) in speech and writing; that is, knowing how to say what one wishes to say. He asserts that for language to be good, it must be clear, or else it 'will not perform its proper function' (1404b). In his comments on the value of metaphor, Aristotle offers some critical advice for achieving dignified airs in one's language, but the use of metaphor is always to be done moderately and in the interest of conveying one's meaning all the more effectively. For this is, as he says, the 'chief merit of rhetorical language' (*hē tou rhētorikou logou aretē*; 1405a1). He contrasts clarity of speech and ingenuity in thought with the sophistic use of synonyms for crafty or deceptive purposes (1404b37-39). In chapter 5, Aristotle states his view that ambiguity is an offense against the good style which equates with purity and correctness in language. He suggests as a general rule that one avoid ambiguities, that is, 'unless you deliberately intend the opposite, like those who, having nothing to say yet pretend to say something' (1407a32-34). He then proceeds to talk about the esoteric ambiguity or obscurity used by the philosophers, Empedocles and Heraclitus.

Ambiguity and the Stoics

Galen, in the second century CE, develops a theory of fallacy, which includes his account of ambiguity in *De Captionibus*, in accordance with his reading of Aristotle's *Sophistici Elenchi*.[7] Galen has a strongly negative, polemical attitude towards Stoic doctrine and he is especially critical of Chrysippus' use of language. His book, however, provides a source for the Stoic view of ambiguity. Diogenes Laertius' doxography is also a primary source on the Stoics. He reports their definition of ambiguity, as follows:

> Verbal ambiguity arises when a word properly, rightfully, and in accordance with fixed usage denotes two or more different things, so that at one and the same time we may take it in several distinct senses signifying two or even more things signifying them verbally, strictly, and in conformity with the same usage, so that at the same time this discourse may be taken in several senses.[8]

According to Catherine Atherton, the Stoic study of ambiguity did not involve an effort to systematize all types of ambiguity. Their interest in ambiguity stems from their theory of dialectic, and goes beyond the concern to explain certain fallacies which are caused by ambiguity, and the attempt to resolve them.[9] Stoic dialectic is not restricted to formal debate nor is it conceived as a mere technical discipline or collection of skills. Diogenes says that the Stoics' view of dialectic is that it is 'indispensable and is itself a virtue, embracing other particular virtues under it'.[10] The Stoics have a global view of philosophy and advocate a way of life in which the studies of physics, ethics and logic are tightly bound and consistently maintained. Their concern with the use of ambiguity is a moral concern, in particular, a concern for dialectical education, and especially with making sure that one has control over those impressions to which one gives one's assent.

In her account of Stoic philosophical ideals, Atherton emphasizes this point. She explains that, on the Stoic view, 'If agents do not realize that an ambiguity in the linguistic expression of a proposition or argument conceals its falsity or unsoundness, or if it leads them to gross misinterpretation, their moral welfare may, in extreme cases, be directly at stake'. The Stoics recognized that making conceptual distinctions in a moral context is especially crucial, 'since here the ambiguity's potential for interference with decision-making would be both grave and manifest'.[11] And further, Atherton says, 'A mistake about concepts induced by a mistake about language may make one's whole life wretched and pointless'.[12]

The Stoics recognized that the intentional use of double meaning, and the mental exercise required by the disambiguation process, were beneficial to philosophers. The constructive use of ambiguity in speech draws attention to various mental associations, and a speaker may wish to emphasize such associations for pedagogical purposes, either because the two meanings of an expression are related in an unconventional way or because the meanings need to be clarified and kept distinct. The Stoics believed in what Atherton refers to as the 'basic rationality of language'; they regarded particular ambiguities as 'throwing useful light on important conceptual connections once their meanings are carefully distinguished'.[13] Atherton also emphasizes the Stoics' interest in the practice of contextual disambiguation. They recognized that in judging whether a term is ambiguous, the relevant context must be considered. Further, she points out that there are systematic differences between the Stoic, non-standard usage and standard usage of certain terms, such as 'good', 'luck' and 'chance'; they were taken to task for failing 'to preserve anything of ordinary usage but the words themselves'.[14]

Aristotle and Galen take a diagnostic approach to ambiguity and consider it mostly in relation to false reasoning and sophistic speech. The Stoics have a wider interest in understanding the problem of ambiguous language which they conceive more thoroughly at the theoretical and practical levels. As we have seen, Plato shares the critical or theoretical approach, and sees language use and misuse as a matter for individual, moral and social concern. He has, however, another interest as a literary writer, and his fascination with the power of ambiguous language extends well beyond the limits of philosophical argumentation, narrowly construed.

Creative Use of Ambiguity

Plato's dialogues are filled with the dramatic interplay of words and speeches. His creative use of language ranks along with the Old Comedy of Aristophanes who relies upon puns, riddles and other wordplay for humorous effect, and with the tragic poetry of Sophocles and Euripides whose works are often analysed for their brilliant and subtle use of double meaning. Classicists, such as W. B. Stanford, Simon Goldhill, Jean-Pierre Vernant and Pierre Vidal-Naquet, recognize the tremendous literary value that the use of ambiguous language has in enhancing the meaning of a poet's expressions, and have discussed the relevance of ambiguity in interpreting Greek tragedy.[15]

According to Stanford, the use of ambiguity originates with Homer and extends to the tragic poets who created an artistic effect known as 'dramatic' or 'tragic' irony. In particular, Sophocles and Euripides use dramatic irony which relies upon there being two senses of a term or phrase. The characters are sometimes made to utter words which are understood with one meaning while a second meaning is conveyed to the audience that bears directly on the action or situation in the play. 'As a literary device', Stanford says, 'an ambiguity is used for the very purpose of expressing more than one meaning ... A writer finds that a certain word has in its traditional use two, or a suggestion of two, distinct meanings which both happen to be congruous in the situation in hand'.[16]

Stanford suggests four possible explanations for why a writer/dramatist would use ambiguity deliberately: (i) to show off 'verbal dexterity' and impress the audience; (ii) to appeal to the etymology of language in constructing an argument; (iii) to suggest hidden meanings, spark the imagination, or affect the emotions of the audience; and (iv) to mislead or deceive the audience, or more likely, as Stanford notes, to show how others are deceived. While this range of usage shows that ambiguity in language has a place and function which is valuable for several purposes, it is typically thought to be no more than a clever means of deception, used by politicians and schoolboys alike, to avoid speaking the truth or to manipulate others. This is the usual basis for condemning the deliberate use of ambiguity as immoral.[17]

Stanford's concern, however, is to offer other alternatives in which ambiguous speech can be used without bringing in the idea of deception. The first use is easily understood as a matter of rhetorical display or sophistic argumentation. For instance, Agathon's speech in praise of Erōs contains verbal fallacies in an attempt to show that Erōs has all the virtues, and this is combined with embellished, poetic versification in the style of Gorgias (*Sym.* 199a-201d).[18] Another example is Prodicus, the Sophist, who is well-known for his ability to distinguish the subtle nuances in terminology.[19] Socrates appeals to Prodicus' skill on several occasions, one of which is most memorable, in the *Protagoras*, where Socrates explains that he is corrected regularly by Prodicus for misusing the word '*deinos*' as 'awful' by applying it to things which are good.[20]

The extended episode where Socrates is required to interpret Simonides' poem and defend his reading is comical and raises a number of linguistic issues (335d-348c). In this passage, Socrates repeats the word '*deinos*' with the phrases that caused the trouble, for example 'awful peace', 'awful health', 'awful wealth' (341b-c). Socrates asks Prodicus for his advice on what Simonides meant in criticizing Pittacus. Prodicus glibly says he thinks that Simonides was 'reproaching Pittacus for not knowing how to distinguish words correctly' (341c6-7).

The etymological use of ambiguity is quite prevalent in Greek literature where the names of characters are appropriately descriptive of them or their life, for example Ajax (*aias* = lament/woe); Pentheus (grief); Helen (destroyer). Stanford remarks that 'these plays on names may be properly described as ambiguities because they always involve a double use of a word or name as a descriptive term as well as a mere demonstrative symbol'.[21] Plato shares in these dramatic techniques. He puns on his character's names, for instance, Polus is an impulsive 'colt'; Polemarchus is a 'war-leader'; Euthyphro's proposed definitions go round in circles and his name means 'straight-thinker'; and Thrasymachus is belligerent and reactive. He is a Sophist known for his ability to arouse the emotions of his audience and his name means 'bold-fighter'.[22]

Besides the fun with ambiguities dramatized in the *Euthydemus*, the *Cratylus* provides a sample of Plato's art of wordplay and his abiding interest in etymology. Two opposing views about the origins and correctness of language are presented and refuted; the conventional view is taken by Hermogenes that words and their referents are the product of convention and nothing more while Cratylus argues for the extreme Heraclitean position that the meanings of words are based in reality and reveal the nature of things.

In the middle of the dialogue, Socrates goes on an excursion in etymological analysis.[23] He traces names back to their possible origin of meaning with humor and fanciful speculation. At the same time, the correctness of many words is critically examined. In the main section devoted to the etymologies, Socrates and Hermogenes investigate the meaning of body and soul (399d-400d) and the names of the gods and goddesses (400d-407d). They also examine knowledge terminology (411a-412c); justice and the other virtue terms (412d-414b); *technē* (414b-415a); and they come to the 'summit' of the inquiry when they focus on the words for virtue, benefit and harm, the noble and the disgraceful (415a-418a).

A reader might tend to dismiss these playful jibes as so much unnecessary mockery, but because the attributes of the interlocutor's character are sometimes built into the argument used to refute him, it is not so simple.[24] The significance can be seen with regard to the brief refutation of the tragic poet, Agathon (*Sym.* 199a-201d). Agathon's name means 'good' (*agathos*), or one might think, a 'good man'. Socrates' argument against him concludes that Erōs lacks beauty and goodness. Agathon had just given a rhetorically inspired speech before the refutation in which he practically identified himself with Erōs, describing the god as a young poet (195a-198a).

The next two types of ambiguity Stanford mentions are related to each other. They explain what philosophers and poets attempt to do when they make use of language which has multiple meanings that are difficult to disambiguate. Esoteric ambiguity is used in cases in which one might deliberately attempt to conceal a meaning from some people and to convey

a private message to others. This type of indirect communication is associated with the obscure sayings and double meanings of the Delphic oracle
and the enigmas of Heraclitus. Socrates approaches the interlocutor's
responses as riddles, as shown earlier with Polemarchus. At the beginning
of the *Cratylus*, Hermogenes asks Socrates if he would 'interpret Cratylus'
oracular speech' (384a7); hidden meanings are associated with Heraclitus
and Protagoras (*Tht.* 152c, 155d-e, 180c-d).

The final type of ambiguity is called 'tragic ambiguity' since the tragedians use it precisely to make a point with their audiences about how
easily people are fooled by words, their own and those of others, and what
the consequences of such misconceptions might be. Sophocles' *Oedipus Tyr-
annos* is a prime example of tragic ambiguity since Oedipus had proudly
solved the riddle of the Sphinx but could not comprehend the oracle's pro-
nouncement with regard to his own life. The speech which Ajax gives before
his suicide, known as the 'deception speech', is packed with ambiguous language and fools Tecmessa and the Chorus into thinking Ajax had changed
his mind (646–65). The words that Dionysus the Stranger speaks to
Pentheus and his replies, in Euripides' *Bacchae*, are double-edged right up
until the moment of Pentheus's death (955–70). *The Stranger*: 'You will
indeed be in your mother's arms'.[25] The tragedians use the ambiguity of language to show their audience the serious consequences of mistaken judgments and the careless use of language and thought.

Socrates uses ambiguity constructively in the dialectic and Plato uses
ambiguity creatively in the dialogues. Their purposes are parallel to each
other: one operates at the dramatic level and the other operates at the textual level. Socrates' use of ambiguity is connected with the elenctic and
protreptic functions, and involves his efforts to reform the interlocutor's thinking by conceptual reorientation. He tries to move the interlocutor
towards his meaning of concepts while staying on common ground with the
interlocutor and using, or appearing to use, the ordinary meaning of words.
Plato is drawing the reader's attention to the philosophical question of
what the correct or best interpretation is of a term or a premise, given the
possible range of meanings available. Like the tragic and comic poets,
Plato is holding the spotlight on the inherent obscurity and interminable
confusion in the ordinary use of value terminology.

Perspectives on Refutation

The deliberate uses of ambiguity in the poetic and sophistic traditions,
and Plato's involvement in these traditions, present the reader with an

alternative perspective on the dialectical strategies of Socratic refutations. The cross-sections between traditions lend credibility to the idea that Plato's dramatic skills and intentions affect the argumentation and that certain fallacies are customized to fit the interlocutor's personal character. None the less, some readers may reject such appeals to Plato's 'literary' side and insist that the arguments stand on their own merit.

From a formalist point of view, the only relevant standards for constructing and evaluating arguments are the logical standards of validity and soundness.[26] The occurrence of ambiguity is a negative and undesirable feature in any context in which argumentation is used. The rules of deductive logic are designed to preserve the truth of the premises in reasoning from the premises to a conclusion, and the preservation of truth is the aim of all reasoning. This single aim is assumed and projected on to Socrates and Plato such that any argumentative strategy they use which violates the rules of logic and interferes with the aim is considered fallacious. The deliberate use of fallacious arguments constitutes unfair practice and deception, and there is little or no regard for any other purposes the arguments may serve.[27]

This position reflects Aristotle's view, for the most part, yet it is clear that he works with the notion of a refutation in a dialectical format. In this format, the deliberate use of fallacy implies deception because a fallacious argument is put forth as if it were valid, presumably in order to trick the opponent. It is difficult to reconcile Aristotle's allegiance to sound logic and unambiguous language with the attitudes that he is compelled to adopt with regard to the dialectical games. But whatever the case may be, Aristotle and the Stoics clearly recognize the value of the tactics that are necessary to refute and avoid being refuted; one is expected to make distinctions and it is part of the exercise to develop the skills that are necessary to defend one's position in debate.

To stay rigidly within the formal limitations of argument is to misunderstand the dialectical context completely. In a dialectical context, there are rules other than those of deductive logic. It seems to be the case that, in constructing an elenctic argument, Socrates is not required to state openly the possible ambiguity of a term that would cause the argument to be invalid. And it seems to be the interlocutor's job to identify and clarify a possible ambiguity if he hopes to avoid being refuted. I have argued that Socrates makes free use of ambiguity and deliberately commits the fallacy of equivocation, among other fallacies, as part of his protreptic strategy. According to Aristotle's typology, many of Socrates' refutations fall under the broader heading of 'irrelevant conclusion', or to put it differently, to suit the Socratic version of the fallacy: showing the Socratic interlocutor his ignorance of what a refutation is. I have also argued that Socratic use of ambiguity is constructive, and that the elenctic discourse is in close partnership with the Socratic protreptic, both of which are goal-directed modes of discourse which aim at moral self-improvement. In light of Socrates' moral aim and his protreptic discourse, Plato's repeated theme of 'knowing how to use' makes the most sense. The difference between Socrates and the Sophists is not only a difference in aims but a difference in their respective uses of fallacies and rhetorical techniques. This is the point of relevance in holding Socrates' moral position to his methodology.

The Normative Use of Technique

As I discussed earlier, there are numerous fallacies or techniques of sophistical refutation which Aristotle has examined.[28] A demonstration of a rhetorical type of refutation is shown, in the *Gorgias*, with Polus, whose courtroom style includes the appeal to witnesses, to popular opinion, to ridicule and to the emotions as the means for refuting an opponent, and for winning approval of the audience.[29] The rhetorical means of persuasion involve argumentative, stylistic and strategic techniques. Techniques of style have to do with the arrangement of words and phrases to affect the listener's emotions and with the quality of delivery.[30] Techniques of strategy have to do with how the speaker is received by the audience and with posturing in order to gain the trust of the audience. In general, sophistic rhetoric is a long and eloquent form of speech-making that is used for display purposes or teaching style. The speeches often take the form of blame and praise and the topics are the stock of commonplaces or those that are taken from mythology. Gorgias' rhetorical art sets the paradigm for the genre. His method employs argumentative, strategic and exaggerated verbal styles of speech, for example rhythm, meter, tone, periphrasis, chiasmus, anaphora, allusion, alliteration. His techniques of persuasion appeal to the aesthetic sensibilities of the listening audience and are meant to entertain and charm them, or move them in whatever way he wishes to do.

Based on the dramatic context of the dialogues, and the historical background available on the Sophists, both Socrates and the Sophists are innovative intellectuals who appeared to talk about the same subjects, and were concerned about virtue and education of the young. Though Aristophanes presents a distorted picture of Socrates for the purposes of comedy and the criticism of intellectual pretense, he is nevertheless an important source for understanding the atmosphere and attitudes of the populace towards the new education (*paideia*).[31]

There are important differences in the Socratic and Sophistic views and their approaches to teaching. In his Great Speech, Protagoras describes the traditional Athenian education as a system of discipline with reward and punishment, schooling in music, the learning of letters and the memorization of poetry (*Prt.* 324d-328d). Just at the start of the episode in which Protagoras will put questions to Socrates about the meaning of Simonides' poem, Protagoras says that 'the greatest part of a man's education is to be skillful in the matter of verses' (339a1-3). Socrates makes a mockery of the practice of literary interpretation but is still able to incorporate a few of his own principles into the meaning of the poem. As the transition back to the dialectical mode of question and answer takes place, Socrates remarks that 'arguing about poetry is comparable to the wine-parties of the common market folk' and shows a 'lack of education' (*apaideusias*; 347d3). As educators, there is some overlap between SM and that the rhetorical techniques and methods of the Sophists that includes a question and answer session, but there are differences in how the questions are asked and answered. Socrates conducts the dialectic with specific questions that lead the interlocutor through serious moral issues which challenge his conventional views. The Sophists do no such thing.[32]

There are strong contrasts between methods at the normative level of use. The distinction is not simply a matter of picking out techniques of argument or other dialectical devices which the Sophists use and Socrates does not, but more a matter of how Socrates uses techniques and devices as opposed to how the Sophists use them. It is too easy to assimilate the technique itself, which is a tool, with the use of that technique, which concerns the good that it produces and the intention of the user. But this distinction is an important one to maintain in understanding SM. The differences that can be identified at the normative level of the use of technique match the differences in the theoretical outlooks of Socrates and the Sophists. The aims and presuppositions direct the use of the techniques and the use is what calls for moral judgment. The techniques are simply the means and are morally neutral. For the most part, how Socrates uses the techniques in the argumentation is vastly different from anything the Sophist tries to do. Socrates questions the interlocutor and hopes to improve him morally; he seeks after the essence of a moral concept; he insists on the sincerity and integrity of the interlocutor; he allows the interlocutor to take back his agreement; and he shows concern for the welfare of the interlocutor's soul with respect to self-knowledge. In these ways, SM is nothing like the sophistic method.

The use that is made of argumentation and the attitude towards the value of the argumentation is determined by a person's character and beliefs, so the method, considered as a whole, that incorporates such argumentation will also be the product of character and beliefs.[33] Keeping this in mind, three distinct methods can be discerned. There is the eristic method, and the eristic use of techniques of argument, which are contentiously employed to win a debate regardless of what is true.[34] There is rhetorical method (base rhetoric), and the use of techniques of argument and poetic devices, which prove effective in gratifying the emotions of the audience. And there is dialectical method (noble rhetoric), and the use of techniques of argument, which are employed to benefit the interlocutor morally by finding out what is true about the greatest matters in life (*Grg.* 500c-d).

The method, and how a man uses the means of argumentation to achieve the results he desires, is not something that is separable from the character of the man who uses it. Techniques of argument are value-neutral means which can be used for good or bad, and it is possible to detach the techniques which serve Socrates and the Sophists from their respective methods. The general point of this analysis is that 'method' is clearly more than a set of means. And so, the method cannot be detached from the man, though the means can. The means of argumentation are neither good nor bad, neither right nor wrong, in themselves. They are such only in relation to their end. The method, however, contains both the means and the aim, plus the presuppositions. The means of argumentation are available to Socrates, the Sophists or anyone else who wants to use them. It is Socrates' use of the means that is central to any normative questions about the value of the method, and his use stems from his character and moral purpose, which are reflected in his philosophical views about wisdom, virtue and human nature.

With specific regard to the use of ambiguity, the difference between the sophistic and Socratic method is that there is a beneficial, philosophical insight, of a protreptic nature, to be gained in recognizing how Socrates uses double meanings. No such connection is intended by the Sophists; there is no attempt to facilitate learning, or to discover the truth. Their concern is with words and the power of words and not with the reality behind the words. The main lesson to be learned from the *Euthydemus* is that apparent contradictions are often the result of equivocation, false dilemmas and *secundum quid*. Although the equivocations used by the brothers are silly and pointless, there are equivocations of a more subtle and serious kind that should be recognized and handled, especially in moral thinking. To be charged with sophistry, Socrates would have to use dialectical techniques to mislead the interlocutor with the intention to deceive or harm, for the sole purpose of winning the debate, or to appear to be wise. Regardless of how much ironical play there is in some of Socrates' conduct and remarks, his intentions are not sophistic. He does not engage in the exploitation of ambiguity to deceive, to win a debate or to gain approval from the audience. He uses ambiguity with considerable care and for moral reasons.

Dialectical Conduct and Conflict

The dialectical conduct which accompanies the elenctic function is clearly adversarial, and this makes it difficult to reconcile the elenctic with the epistemic function at the practical level; by 'practical' I mean: what are the results, whom does he persuade, how fair is he to the interlocutors, and how well does he represent philosophy to those he seeks to persuade. The purpose of SM is for Socrates to make himself and the interlocutor better men, with respect to self-knowledge. Socrates is aware that the interlocutor may perceive things differently, and he may be right to think that the two functions do not conflict with one another, in principle. But if they are mixed together indiscriminately, then the interlocutor's expectations are frustrated, procedures are violated and confusion or anger results. Socrates' irony does not alleviate the problem but makes it worse since it often conveys a transparently superior attitude.

The question and answer format of Socratic dialectic appears to be a contest or *agōn*. The appearance is obviously the case when Socrates engages with the Sophists, who see every discussion as an opportunity to debate and win approval from the audience. Despite Socrates' disclaimers, a refutation is closely related to the debate style of an *agōn* and it is easily confused with, and can degenerate into, an eristic or quarrelsome discourse. In his response to Socrates' request that he keep his answers short, Protagoras tells Socrates: 'I have undertaken in my time many contests of speech ...' (*agōna logōn*, 335a4). When Gorgias makes his reply to Socrates about what the 'power of his art' can do, he says: 'At the same time, Socrates, our use of rhetoric should be like our use of any other sort of exercise' (*agōnia*, 456d1). Throughout Gorgias' speech, he compares his art to the athletic exercises and contests of wrestling or boxing, and he draws a parallel to them in order to plead his case that such skills must be 'used fairly' (*dikaiōs chrēsthai*, 456e3). Socrates questions Thrasymachus about his critical remarks on Socrates' manner and Thrasymachus says 'for you won't get the better of me by stealth and, failing stealth, you are not of the force to beat me in debate' (*Rep.* I 341b1-2).

Truth-seeking is one of the functions of SM, but in a dialectical context where refutation is also a function, truth-seeking is subordinate and indirect, and it does not alter or eliminate the adversarial atmosphere. Socrates claims to be seeking truth, yet as Callicles points out, Socrates also seems to be using verbal tricks (*sophisms*) to refute him (*Grg.* 482e4-7; cf. 497a6). Such tactics are thought to be incompatible with the claim to seek truth.[35] Callicles complains to Gorgias that Socrates 'keeps on asking petty, unimportant questions until he refutes one' (497b5–7). Gorgias replies, 'Why, what does that matter to you? In any case it is not your credit that is at stake, Callicles; just permit Socrates to refute you in such manner as he chooses' (497b8-10).

In the long, heated scene with Callicles (480d-523a), Socrates seems oblivious to the psychological disparity between the two modes of discourse. The drama shows that Socrates is driven by the rationality of the argument, the power of the *logos*. He feels the need to complete the argument, so that it may, as he says, 'pick up a head' (505d2). Callicles is at his wits' end and virtually calls Socrates a 'tyrant' in discussion: 'How overbearing (*biaios*) you are, Socrates', and asks him to 'let this argument drop, or find some one else to argue with' (505d5-8). Socrates will pursue the argument to the end by himself, if the rest of the company agree. At a timely moment, Gorgias consents and Socrates monologues with himself, in a manner as he would with any other interlocutor.

There are a number of points which I think both Socrates, as the character portrayed in the dialogues, and Plato as the author, believe with regard to SM. First, SM is a therapeutic process. Socrates is the practitioner in a very difficult line of work who must administer a sort of purification that is necessary to get rid of false conceit, in most cases (cf. *Soph.* 230c-d). Secondly, as a matter of dramatic structure, the *aporiai* are beneficial and help set up the problems to be discussed. Thirdly, in principle, the three modes of discourse and their immediate goals are compatible with each other when understood properly and serve a single aim of moral self-improvement. Fourthly, despite its limitations, the potential benefits of SM are worth the trouble, even if there is the likelihood of falling into an eristic style of debate.

Be that as it may, there remains a sense of disappointment and failure with the endings of the dialogues seem to have nothing to do with *aporia*, and everything to do with Socrates' method and his character, to the degree that they represent the life and death of the historical Socrates. The disturbing feelings clearly arise with regard to the *Gorgias* and quite naturally at the end of the *Phaedo* and *Crito*. Other scenes conjure up similar feelings, for example the episode with Anytus in the *Meno* and Alcibiades' emotional speech in the *Symposium*; even at the end of the *Euthydemus* for all its comic satire, one may share the experience of Crito who is not sure why Socrates engages with such foolish people.

The Drama and the Method

It seems that the less satisfied one is with the apparently unsuccessful results of SM, the more inclined one may be to look for other ways to account for the use of fallacy and other distasteful conduct on the part of Socrates. There are at least two ways to go: one is to think that Plato not only recognized the flaws and implicitly criticized SM, but that he abandoned it, or transformed it into the philosophically promising methods of hypothesis and division which have new metaphysical and epistemological groundings. Another way to go is to take the drama of the dialogues as relevant to Plato's motivations, and study the dramatic cues for an explanation in terms of his artistic and pedagogical purposes. Hopefully, by now, it is clear that I favor the second approach. This approach, which I hesitate to label, honors the Greek literary tradition to which Plato belonged and interprets the dialogues as a philosophical form of drama; it is a unique genre with the poetic elements of tragedy, comedy, epic and rhetoric.[36] Plato's dialogues are artworks. They are visionary and imaginative. His art is to combine these poetic elements and his understanding of Greek culture and its history with Socrates' philosophical conversations and all the tension of opposites that comes with the tragic/comic character of Socrates.

Notes

Chapter 1: The Socratic Method of Dialectic

1. There are a handful of recent, and not so recent, scholars who offer accounts of Socratic dialectic, and/or have literary-based approaches to the Platonic dialogues, which are similar to mine. These include H. L. Sinaiko, *Love, Knowledge, and Discourse in Plato: Dialogue and Dialectic in Phaedrus, Republic, Parmenides* (Chicago: University of Chicago Press, 1965); R. H. Weingartner, *The Unity of the Platonic Dialogue* (Indianapolis: Bobbs-Merrill, 1973); H.G. Gadamer, *Dialogue and Dialectic: Eight Hermeneutical Studies on Plato*, trans. P. Christopher Smith (New Haven and London: Yale University Press, 1980); H. Teloh, *Socratic Education in Plato's Early Dialogues* (Notre Dame: Notre Dame University Press, 1986); R. B. Rutherford, *The Art of Plato: Ten Essays in Platonic Interpretation* (Cambridge, MA: Harvard University Press, 1995); F. Gonzalez, *Dialectic and Dialogue: Plato's Practice of Philosophical Inquiry* (Evanston: Northwestern University Press, 1998); G. A. Scott, *Plato's Socrates as Educator* (Albany: State University of New York Press, 2000); J. Gordon, *Turning Toward Philosophy: Literary Device and Dramatic Structure in Plato's Dialogues* (University Park: Pennsylvania State University Press, 1999).

2. Unless otherwise indicated, all translations of the texts are taken from *The Loeb Classical Library* (London: Heinemann and Cambridge, MA: Harvard University Press). For information on translations, see the bibliography.

3. R. Robinson, *Plato's Earlier Dialectic* (Oxford: Oxford University Press, 1953); G. Vlastos, 'The Socratic Elenchus', *Oxford Studies in Ancient Philosophy* 1 (1983): 27–58, revised and reprinted in *Socratic Studies* as 'The Socratic Elenchus: Method is All', 1–29, with Appendix and Postscript, 29–37, ed. M. Burnyeat (Cambridge: Cambridge University Press, 1994); G. Santas, *Socrates: Philosophy in Plato's Early Dialogues* (London: Routledge and Kegan Paul, 1979); T. H. Irwin, *Plato's Moral Theory* (Oxford: Clarendon Press, 1977) and *Plato's Ethics* (Oxford: Oxford University Press, 1995).

4. Cf. T. Brickhouse and N. D. Smith, *Plato's Socrates* (Oxford: Oxford University Press, 1994); M. McPherran, *The Religion of Socrates* (University Park: Pennsylvania State University Press, 1996); H. H. Benson, *Socratic Wisdom: The Model of Knowledge in Plato's Early Dialogues* (Oxford: Oxford University Press, 2000); J. Beversluis, *Cross-examining Socrates: A Defense of the Interlocutors in Plato's Early Dialogues* (Cambridge: Cambridge University Press, 2000).

5. My views with respect to the current debates on interpretive matters coincide with the scholars, mentioned in note 1, who depart from, or take issue with, those who belong to the 'doctrinal' or 'analytic' tradition of Platonic interpretation mentioned in notes 3 and 4. Scholars from the analytic tradition usually accept a standardized, chronological view of Plato's intellectual development which divides the dialogues into three main groups; they tend to base their interpretations of the dialogues on the arguments in an effort to establish a Platonic set of doctrines; they recognize and emphasize the distinction between Platonic doctrine and the moral-psychological views and methods they attribute to the Platonic Socrates. For a discussion of the issues that separate the non-doctrinal tradition of interpreting Plato from the doctrinal interpretations, see the introductions to the following texts: F. J. Gonzalez (ed.), *The Third Way: New Dimensions in Platonic Studies* (Lanham, MD: Rowman and Littlefield, 1995); Rutherford, *The Art of Plato*; G. Press (ed.), *Who Speaks for Plato?: Studies in Platonic Anonymity* (Lanham, MD: Rowman and Littlefield, 2000); G. A. Scott (ed.), *Does Socrates have a Method? Rethinking the* Elenchus *in Plato's Dialogues and Beyond* (University Park: Pennsylvania State University Press, 2002). See also G. Press, 'The State of the Question in the Study of Plato', *Southern Journal of Philosophy* 34 (1996): 507–32, reprinted in N. D. Smith (ed.), *Plato: Critical Assessments*, vol. 1 (New York: Routledge, 1998). In general, I agree with the views put forward by Gordon, *Turning Toward Philosophy*, 1–17.

6. I give my attention to Vlastos' version of the epistemological model for purposes of contrast and because his approach is well known and open to weaknesses which I can easily address in light of the model I wish to present. This should not be taken to imply that there are no other workable models of SM to discuss. On the contrary, I have been influenced by the educational models offered by H. Teloh, *Socratic Education*, and the educational-erotic model recently offered by G. A. Scott, *Plato's Socrates as Educator*.

7. Vlastos, 'The Socratic Elenchus', 30 and *Socratic Studies*, 4. Henceforward, all references are to the *Socratic Studies* version unless otherwise noted. In this version, the phrase 'question and answer' is inserted to read 'a search for moral truth by question and answer adversary argument', 4. As most Platonic scholars recognize, Vlastos' position on SM is complicated, enormously influential and must be confronted regardless of whether one agrees or disagrees with his overall position. His views on the interpretive issues concerning Socrates and Plato are discussed in *Socrates: Ironist and Moral Philosopher* (Ithaca: Cornell University Press, 1991).

8. See M. McPherran, 'Socratic Piety in the *Euthyphro*', in H. H. Benson (ed.), *Essays on the Philosophy of Socrates* (Oxford: Oxford University Press, 1992), 220–41 and Brickhouse and Smith, *Plato's Socrates*, 64–69 for a discussion of constructivist positions.

9. Cf. Robinson, *Plato's Earlier Dialectic*. See Vlastos' comments, *Socratic Studies*, on the history of Socratic scholarship with regard to the negative characterization of the method before his interpretation, 17–19. Earlier negative accounts of SM

are S. Kierkegaard, *The Concept of Irony with Continual Reference to Socrates*, ed. and trans. H. V. Hong and E. H. Hong (Princeton: Princeton University Press, 1989) and G. Grote, *Plato and Other Companions of Sokrates*, 3 vols., trans. J. Murray (London: J. Murray, 1865).

10.   Vlastos, *Socrates: Ironist*, 14.

11.   *Chrm.* 158d; *La.* 187d; *Cr.* 48d; *Prt.* 348c-e.

12.   Vlastos, *Socratic Studies*, 21.

13.   *Ap.* 29e1-2, 30a-b; *Chrm.* 157a-b; *Eu.* 2c-d; *Grg.* 512e-513a, 515a-d, 520d-e; *La.* 185e-186b, 189e, 190b-c; *Prt.* 318a-e.

14.   Cf. Rutherford, *Art of Plato*, 177; E. R. Dodds (trans.), *Plato: Gorgias* (Oxford: Clarendon Press, 2002 [1959]), 296–98.

15.   A. A. Long, 'Plato's Apologies and Socrates in the *Theaetetus*', 126, in J. Gentzler (ed.), *Method in Ancient Philosophy* (Oxford: Clarendon Press, 1998), 113–36.

16.   H. G. Liddell and R. A. Scott, *Greek-English Lexicon* (Oxford: Oxford University Press, 1985), 105.

17.   As a questioner, Socrates of the *Gorgias* is portrayed as being sensitive to the reactions of his interlocutors. Socrates tells Gorgias, 'It is not you I am after, it is our discussion, to have it proceed in such a way as to make the things we are talking about most clear to us' (453c2-5), and again, 'I am asking questions so that we can conduct an orderly discussion. It is not you I am after; it is to prevent our getting in the habit of second-guessing and snatching each other's statements away ahead of time' (454c2–5, trans. Zeyl).

18.   The main aporetic dialogues and key passages are the following: *Chrm.* 176a-b; *Eu.* 15b-c; *HMaj.* 304c-e; *HMin.* 376c; *La.* 200e; *Ly.* 222e; *Meno* 80a; *Prt.* 361c, and *Rep.* I 354b-c.

19.   In the *Hippias Major,* Hippias remarks that he could find the answer if he was given time to think about it alone (295a-b, 297d-e). He later attributes the difficulties to Socrates' method of inquiry (301b-d, 304a-b) and to the boorishness of the questioner.

20.   *Cr.* 49d; *HMaj.* 365c-d; *La.* 193c; *Meno* 71d, 83d; *Prt.* 331b-d; *Rep.* I 349a-b; *Tht.* 154c-e.

21.   The topic of sincerity is given great emphasis by Vlastos, *Socrates: Ironist*, 14; *Socratic Studies*, 8–10 following Robinson, *Plato's Earlier Dialectic*, 15–17.

22.   Vlastos, *Socratic Studies*, 9.

23.   The demand for sincerity is not simply an issue for the interlocutor. When Callicles answers a question, admittedly in order to avoid inconsistency, the conversation goes as follows: *Socrates:* You are wrecking your earlier statements, Callicles, and you would no longer be adequately inquiring into the truth of the matter with me if you speak contrary to what you think. *Callicles:* You do it too, Socrates. *Socrates:* In that case, it isn't right for me to do it, if it's what I do, or for you either (495a7-b1, trans. Zeyl).

24.   The translations are from R. Waterfield, *Plato: Theaetetus* (London: Penguin Books, 1987).

25.   Euripides, *Hippolytus*, 612; Aristophanes, *Frogs*, 1471; cf. *Sym.* 199a5-6.

26. Socrates tells Protagoras, 'For although my first object is to test the argument, the result perhaps will be that both I, the questioner, and my respondent are brought to the test' (*Prt.* 333c7-10).
27. Vlastos, *Socratic Studies*, 23–24; cf. J. Bailly, 'What you say, what you believe, and what you mean', *Ancient Philosophy* 19 (1999), 65–76; Beversluis, *Cross-examining Socrates*, 37–58.
28. Cf. D. Cairns, Aidōs: *The Psychology and Ethics of Honour and Shame in Ancient Greek Literature* (Oxford: Clarendon Press, 1993); B. Williams, *Shame and Necessity* (Berkeley and Los Angeles: University of California Press, 1993).
29. Each character is portrayed with his own sense of shame, e.g. Gorgias: 455c-d, 461b-c; Polus: 474b-475e, 482e-483a; Callicles: 487b-c, 489b9–10, 494c-e, and Socrates: 508b-c, 522d-e.
30. Cf. G. B. Kerferd, *The Sophistic Movement* (Cambridge: Cambridge University Press, 1981), 111–30.
31. Note that '*aidōs*' translates here, in the *Protagoras*, as 'respect' whereas in the *Charmides*, '*aidōs*' translates as 'modesty' (160e-161b).
32. J. S. Morrison, *Antiphon*, in R. K. Sprague (ed.), *The Older Sophists* (Columbia: University of South Carolina Press, 1972), 106–240; M. Gagarin, *Antiphon the Athenian* (Austin: University of Texas Press, 2002).
33. The adjective '*aischron*' is a derivative of the noun '*aischunē*' and is commonly rendered in English as 'shame' or 'disgrace', though the Greek term has a wider application. The abstract noun in the neuter form '*to aischron*' translates as 'the shameful'. '*Aischunē*' and its cognates are closely tied to the complex range of usages associated with *aidōs*, which translates as 'respect', 'reverence' or 'awe'. Cf. Liddell and Scott, *Greek-English Lexicon*, 23–24.
34. The topic of shame in SM is a delicate fruit that is easily bruised. See C. Kahn, 'Drama and Dialectic in Plato's *Gorgias*', *Oxford Studies in Ancient Philosophy* 1 (1983): 75–121; R. McKim, 'Shame and Truth in Plato's *Gorgias*', in C. Griswold (ed.), *Platonic Writings, Platonic Readings* (New York: Routledge, 1988), 34–48; Beversluis, *Cross-examining Socrates*, 70–71 and *passim*; J. Gordon, *Turning Toward Philosophy*, 22–28; P. Woodruff, 'Socrates and the Irrational', in N.D. Smith and P. Woodruff (eds.), *Reason and Religion in Socratic Philosophy* (Oxford: Oxford University Press, 2000), 130–50.
35. In the *Symposium*, the wish or love for happiness is said to be 'common to all mankind' (*koinon ... panton anthropon*), and the question of whether this is so is put to Socrates, by Diotima, and Socrates agrees (205a7-8, cf. *Rep.* VI 505d10).
36. The identification of 'desire' with 'lack' is central in understanding the protreptic function in the *Lysis* (221e-222b).
37. The superior value of the soul is mentioned explicitly with Hippocrates in the *Protagoras* (313a6), and with *Crito* (47e-48a). Cf. *Grg.* 512a6-7; *Sym.* 210b7; *Rep.* IV 445a9-b3.
38. The topics and issues related to Socrates' conception of the soul and to his views on self-knowledge are given a more thorough treatment in my dissertation, *Socratic*

Method and Self-knowledge in Plato's Early Dialogues (Ann Arbor: University Microfilms, Inc., 1999).

39. Brickhouse and Smith give this approach its most extensive formulation, *Plato's Socrates*, 18–21. See also, *Socrates on Trial* (Princeton: Princeton University Press, 1989), 105–107, where they argue that Socrates' 'confidence in the value of his mission cannot derive from elenctic justification', 105.

40. For critical remarks on Brickhouse and Smith, *Plato's Socrates*, see R. Kraut, 'Critical Review: Brickhouse and Smith's *Plato's Socrates*', *Ancient Philosophy* 15 (1995): 619–45.

41. Although I agree with Brickhouse and Smith, *Plato's Socrates*, that Socrates has strong personal beliefs which are expressed in the *Apology*, and may account for his overriding concern with wisdom, the good of the soul and the soul's connection with the divine, I interpret these beliefs primarily in the context in which they occur in the arguments that are given throughout the early dialogues. I believe that Brickhouse and Smith overstate the role that these personal beliefs have in justifying the SM because they rely too much on the *Apology*. I do not think that such an account goes very far in explaining the value of a philosophical method that supposedly can be used by anyone who wishes to use it, which is one of the particular points that Brickhouse and Smith make. If it is mainly Socrates' personal religious convictions which justify his method, then it does not seem to be the case that 'Any of us *could* do what Socrates does, although, of course, not so well, and, according to Socrates, *all* of us *should* do what he does' (Brickhouse and Smith, *Plato's Socrates*, 10).

Chapter 2: The Proptreptic Function

1. Commentators who have studied the protreptic aspects of SM include: T. Chance, *Plato's* Euthydemus: *Analysis of What Is and Is Not Philosophy* (Berkeley: University of California Press, 1992); D. Roochnik, *Of Art and Wisdom: Plato's Understanding of Techne* (University Park: Pennsylvania State University Press, 1996); S. R. Slings, *Plato: Clitophon* (Cambridge: Cambridge University Press, 1999); F. J. Gonzalez, *Dialectic and Dialogue: Plato's Practice of Philosophical Inquiry* (Evanston: Northwestern University Press, 1998); J. Gordon, *Turning Towards Philosophy: Literary Device and Dramatic Structure in Plato's Dialogues* (University Park: Pennsylvania State University Press, 1999).

2. Cf. M. Burnyeat, 'Fathers and Sons in Plato's *Republic* and *Philebus*', *Classical Quarterly* 54.1 (2004): 80–87.

3. See Burnyeat, 'Fathers and Sons', for references to what he calls 'courage in debate', 82, n. 9.

4. *Ap.* 30a10-b1.

5. *Chrm.* 157a4; *La.* 185e3–4.

6. Slings, *Plato*, 103.

7. In his discussion of happiness, in Book I.8 of the *Nicomachean Ethics*, Aristotle's frequent reference to the current views (*ta endoxa*) in presenting his own account shows the extent to which he depends on what others have said (*tōn legomenōn peri autēs*, 1098b11). On the specific relevance of *ta endoxa* in his moral methodology, see *NE* 1098b25-29 and 1145b1-8.

8. Cf. Protagoras' great speech (*Prt.* 320d-328d).

9. Vlastos claims that the *elenchos* does not rely on *endoxa* for the truth of the premises, *Socratic Studies*, 13–14, *Socrates: Ironist*, 111–13, cf. 94–95. For critical responses, see R. Kraut, 'Comments on Gregory Vlastos, "The Socratic Elenchus"', *Oxford Studies in Ancient Philosophy* 1 (1983): 59–70; R. Polansky, 'Professor Vlastos's Analysis of Socratic Elenchus', *Oxford Studies in Ancient Philosophy* 3 (1985): 247–259; and R. Bolton, 'Aristotle's Account of Socratic Elenchus', *Oxford Studies in Ancient Philosophy* 11 (1993): 121–52.

10. I adopt this distinction from S. Klein, 'The Value of *Endoxa* in Ethical Argument', *History of Philosophical Quarterly* 9.2 (April 1992): 141–57, see esp. 156–57, n. 48.

11. See Kraut, 'Comments', 64, for this example.

12. What I mean by this is that the interlocutor's stated belief is endoxical as long as it is derived from conventional or reputable opinion. If the meaning of '*endoxa*' is taken to preclude the possibility that endoxical beliefs represent the interlocutor's own contribution, then it would make sense to claim that Socrates does not use *endoxa* in his method because Socrates is only concerned with what the interlocutor himself believes. But I do not think that the term should be given a technical or narrow meaning. Aristotle uses it quite broadly in his discussion of dialectic (*Top.* 100a29-b23).

13. Other scholars have noted one or more of these premises in their discussion of Socrates' views. For instance, C. Kahn, 'Drama and Dialectic in Plato's *Gorgias*', *Oxford Studies in Ancient Philosophy* 1 (1983): 75–121, believes that the premise that all humans desire the good is fundamental to understanding the SM. R. McKim, 'Shame and Truth in Plato's *Gorgias*', in C. Griswold (ed.), *Platonic Writings, Platonic Readings* (New York: Routledge, 1988), 34–48, argues that the belief that virtue is beneficial is a Socratic axiom that cannot be denied by the interlocutors successfully. D. Roochnik, 'Socrates' Use of the Techne Analogy', *Journal of the History of Philosophy* 24 (1986): 295–310, claims that the premise that virtue is a *technē* is a dialectical premise that is essential to the *elenchos*. See T. H. Irwin, *Plato's Moral Theory* (Oxford: Clarendon Press, 1977), cf. *Plato's Ethics* (Oxford: Oxford University Press, 1995), 48–50. Irwin identifies a group of premises which he calls 'guiding principles' which are conceived much differently from what I present.

14. Conventional Athenian views about the social benefits and harms of virtue are brought to bear on the question of justice in the dialectic between Socrates, Glaucon and Adeimantus in *Republic* II. An indispensable sourcebook on Greek conventional values and terminology is K. J. Dover, *Greek Popular Morality in the Time of Plato and Aristotle* (Indianapolis: Hackett Publishing Co., 1994 [Oxford: Blackwell, 1974]).

15.   The truth of premise (B) is challenged by Thrasymachus and Callicles. Thrasyma-chus denies the conventional meaning of justice precisely because justice is not beneficial, so Socrates moves to another endoxical premise. Callicles is shown why he cannot deny that temperance is beneficial.

16.   Other implications associated with the premise that virtue is like a *technē* are that each branch of knowledge is individuated by its particular subject matter, and that each knowledge is distinct from what it is a knowledge of (*Chrm.* 165c-166c). Furthermore, each *technē* is mastered as a whole subject (*Ion* 530d-533c).

17.   I say 'roughly' to allow for some overlap. For a similar breakdown of interlocutors, see W. Thomas Schmid's 'Socrates' Practice of Elenchus in the *Charmides*', *Ancient Philosophy* 1 (1981): 141–47, G. A. Scott, Plato's *Socrates as Educator* (Albany: State University of New York Press, 2000), and R. Blondell, *The Play of Character in Plato's Dialogues* (Cambridge: Cambridge University Press, 2002).

18.   See D. Nails, *The People of Plato: A Prosopography of Plato and Other Socratics* (Indiana-polis: Hackett Publishing Co., 2002).

19.   Among the non-sophistic group, there are some interlocutors who exhibit sophistic-like traits, like Ctesippus, Meno and Menexenus. Other non-sophistic interlocutors are older and have minor roles, like Cephalus, Lysimachus and Melesias. Theo-dorus, as a friend of Protagoras, might fit into Group 4; he stubbornly refuses to enter into the dialectic with Socrates, though he gets drawn into it sometimes and plays an active role in the drama. A miscellaneous group might include: Alcibiades, Aristophanes, Crito and Cratylus, who are very dramatic characters and seem unclassifiable. My lists are not intended to be exhaustive.

20.   This premise is uncontroversial and provides an instance of endoxical premise (B) which Socrates also endorses when it is given a Socratic interpretation. The truth of the premise for Cleinias lies in the belief that whatever is good is that which is to his benefit, understood broadly to mean better for his body, his reputation and espe-cially his chances for financial or political success.

21.   See R. K. Sprague, *Plato's Use of Fallacy: A Study of the* Euthydemus *and Some Other Dialogues* (London: Routledge and Kegan Paul, 1962).

22.   Compare this, for instance, to the way that Protagoras responds to Socrates' request to tell Hippocrates what he will learn if he becomes a follower. Protagoras addresses Hippocrates and says, 'Young man, this is what you will get if you study with me: The very day you start, you will go home a better man, and the same thing will happen the day after. Every day, day after day, you will get better and better' (318a8-b2, trans. Lombardo and Bell).

23.   This principle is similar to the one mentioned in the *Euthydemus* (281d-e), and to the one identified as Socratic by Nicias in the *Laches* (184c-d).

24.   For instance, at *Lysis* 221d-222a, the cause of *philia* is said to be desire and desire ori-ginates in a deficiency. Socrates asks, 'The desiring thing desires that in which it is deficient, does it not?' 'Yes.' 'And the deficient is a friend to that in which it is defi-cient?' 'I suppose so'. Socrates then suggests that we are deficient in 'what belongs to us by nature and what belongs to us by nature' is what we need to befriend (222a7). The Socratic view of motivation is reflected in this description of human nature.

25. There are, of course, elenctic features in any discussion in which Socrates questions what the interlocutor knows and shows him his ignorance. The elenctic and pro-treptic functions work hand in hand. By focusing primarily on the protreptic side of the method, I do not mean to imply that the two functions are mutually exclusive in any sense. What I do wish to emphasize, in going over these particular examples, is that in cases where there are non-sophistic interlocutors in Group 1, Socrates' line of argument is fairly straightforward, and represents his moral position to a large extent.

Chapter 3: Ambiguity and Argumentation

1. Commentators often recognize a strong bifurcation between the 'elenctic' and the 'constructive' Socrates. See R. Blondell, *The Play of Character in Plato's Dialogues* (Cambridge: Cambridge University Press, 2002), 12–14.

2. H. G. Gadamer speaks of Socrates as the 'master of logical traps' who gets himself caught up and allows himself to be 'carried along by language and the ambiguities that it contains'; *Plato's Dialectical Ethics: Phenomenological Interpretations Relating to the Philebus*, trans. R. M. Wallace (New Haven and London: Yale University Press, 1983), 57.

3. Aristophanes, *The Frogs* 1490–1500. Translated by B. B. Rogers (London: Heine-mann; and Cambridge, MA: Harvard University Press, 1924), 433–35.

4. C. Collard, 'Formal Debates in Euripides' Drama', *Greece and Rome* 22 (1975): 58–71; H. G. Wolz, 'Philosophy as Drama: An Approach to Plato's Dialogues', *International Philosophical Quarterly* 3 (1963): 236–70.

5. S. Goldhill, *Reading Greek Tragedy* (Cambridge: Cambridge University Press, 1986), 232–33.

6. F. J. Gonzalez, *Dialectic and Dialogue: Plato's Practice of Philosophical Inquiry* (Evanston: Northwestern University Press, 1998). For discussion, see especially Chapters 6 and 7.

7. Cf. the passage on misology (*Phd.* 89d-91c) and *Rep.* VII (537c-e).

8. J. Kooij, *Ambiguity in Natural Language* (Amsterdam: North-Holland Publishing, 1971), defines 'ambiguity' as 'that property of a sentence that it can be interpreted in more than one way', 5; C. Atherton, *The Stoics on Ambiguity* (Cambridge: Cambridge University Press, 1993), gives a description of ambiguity, rather than a strict definition, which she says is 'deliberately imprecise', and broad enough to cover lexical and syntactic ambiguity. Ambiguity 'is a property of linguistic items such that these items have more than one definite and specific use, meaning, interpretation, etc.', 16.

9. *Grg.* 452e1-2, 454b-c, 488b1-c, 489b-d; *Meno*, 77c-d.

10. *Chrm.* 163d-e.

11. G. A. Scott, *Plato's Socrates as Educator* (Albany: State University of New York Press, 2000), 15–23. Scott notes, '[P]erhaps Socrates would accept that he is an educator

if one means something quite different than would have been connoted by the term *didaskalos*', 16.

12.   Aristotle, *SE* 165b25–166a5. Aristotle's work in this text and in the *Topics* is relevant to any critical discussion on eristic or sophistical reasoning, ambiguity and fallacies, which I discuss in detail in Chapter 4. See R. K. Sprague, 'Logic and Literary Form in Plato', *The Personalist* 48 (1967): 560–72; cf. idem, *Plato's Use of Fallacy: A Study of the* Euthydemus *and Some Other Dialogues* (London: Routledge & Kegan Paul, 1962).

13.   Gonzalez, *Dialectic and Dialogue*, 99–100.

14.   Gonzalez, *Dialectic and Dialogue*, 100.

15.   Gonzalez, *Dialectic and Dialogue*, 103.

16.   See W. R. M. Lamb's note on this passage: 'here the apparent quibble of εὖ πράττειν ('act well' and 'fare well') is intended to suggest a real dependence of happiness upon virtue' (468–69). According to E. R. Dodds, *Plato: Gorgias* (Oxford: Oxford University Press, 1959), 335–36, 'Plato has taken advantage of the convenient ambiguity of εὖ πράττειν. This phrase, and others of the same type, normally have the 'passive' sense of 'faring well'; but they can also be used of action'. Dodds notes that 'Plato exploits the same ambiguity' at *Charmides* 172a2-4. Dodds believes that Plato was not unaware of the ambiguity of the term. He says that the ambiguity is again 'called into play' at *Rep.* I 353e-354a and *Alc.* I 116b, and claims that Plato deliberately used εὖ πράττωμεν with a double meaning, at the end of the *Republic* (621d3).

17.   In his commentary at 172a2-4, T. G. Tuckey says, 'Indeed, it was only by a sophism that technical perfection became identified with happiness in 172a, since it was first stated there that the inhabitants of the infallible society would necessarily εὖ πράττειν and then that, as εὖ πράττοντες, they must be εὐδαίμόνες' (*Plato's Charmides*, Cambridge: Cambridge University Press, 1951), 74.

18.   R. S. W. Hawtrey, *Commentary on Plato's* Euthydemus (Philadelphia: American Philosophical Society, 1981), 77–78, 84, 90. Regarding the ambiguity of '*eu prattein*' at *Eud.* 278e3 and 282a1, see Sprague, *Plato's Use of Fallacy*, 10; T. Irwin, 'Socratic Puzzles', *Oxford Studies in Ancient Philosophy* 10 (1992): 241–66, esp. 259–60; T. Brickhouse and N. Smith, *Plato's Socrates* (Oxford: Oxford University Press, 1994), 113, n. 7; Gonzalez, *Dialectic and Dialogue*, 94–128; T. Chance, *Plato's* Euthydemus*: Analysis of What Is and Is Not Philosophy* (Berkeley: University of California Press, 1992), 65, 239, n. 36.

19.   Hawtrey, *Commentary on Plato's* Euthydemus, 78.

20.   See the debate between M. A. Stewart and R. K. Sprague, in the set of articles called 'Plato's Sophistry', *The Aristotelian Society*, 51, Supp. (1977): 21–44, 45–61.

21.   Hawtrey, *Commentary on Plato's* Euthydemus, 90.

22.   Cf. G. Klosko, 'Toward a Consistent Interpretation of the *Protagoras*', *Archiv für Geschichte der Philosophie* 61 (1975): 125–42.

23.   M. Gifford, 'Dramatic Dialectic in *Republic* Book I', *Oxford Studies in Ancient Philosophy* 20 (Summer 2001): 35–106, see especially 85–91.

24.   The point is made in note c by Shorey, 30–31.

25. See R. C. Cross and A. D. Woozley, *Plato's Republic: A Philosophical Commentary* (London: Macmillan, 1964), especially 21–22; D. J. Allan (trans.), *Plato: Republic Book I* (London: Methuen, 1953), especially note on 335b6, 91; A. Jeffrey, 'Polemarchus and Socrates on Justice and Harm' *Phronesis* 24.1 (1979): 54–69; J. Annas, *An Introduction to Plato's Republic* (New York: Oxford University Press, 1981); J. Beversluis, *Cross-examining Socrates: A Defense of the Interlocutors in Plato's Early Dialogues* (Cambridge: Cambridge University Press, 2000), 203–220; see Gifford, 'Dramatic Dialectic', for criticisms of Beversluis' position, 79, n. 61; 86, n. 68.

26. Socrates is very familiar with the conventional view about benefits and harms. For instance, in the *Eud.* (279a-c); *Grg.* (467e2-3); *Meno* (87e); *Ap.* (36b8-10, cf. 35a-b); *Cr.* (46c1-5, 48b1-2). In the *Gorgias*, Polus mentions such harms as being put to death, having one's property confiscated and being banished from the city (466c-d). In a later discussion at 511a, Callicles reminds Socrates that despite Socrates' claims that the tyrannical ruler is miserable and friendless, such a ruler can put people to death and take their property. Socrates says, 'I do know that, Callicles. I'm not deaf. I hear you say it, and heard Polus just now say it many times, and just about everyone else in the city' (511b1-3, trans. Zeyl).

27. A note to this effect occurs in G. M. A. Grube's translation, *Plato's Republic*, revised by C.D.C. Reeve (Indianapolis: Hackett Publishing Co., 1992), 10, n. 12. Grube/Reeve supplies references to the following texts: *Chrm.* 161a8–9; *Eu.* 6d9-e1; *Grg.* 506d2-4; *Prt.* 332b4-6; *Rep.* I 353d9-354a2.

28. Cf. H. S. Thayer, 'Plato: The Theory and Language of Function', in A. Sesonske (ed.), *Plato's Republic: Interpretation and Criticism* (Belmont: Wadsworth Publishing Co., 1966), 21–39.

29. Cf. *Prt.* 329d-333b on the reciprocity principle of powers. See J. Zembaty, 'Socrates' Perplexity in Plato's *Hippias Minor*', in J. Anton and A. Preus (eds), *Essays in Greek Philosophy* III (Albany: State University of New York Press, 1989), 51–70; M. Burnyeat, 'Virtues in Action', in G. Vlastos (ed.), *Plato: A Collection of Critical Essays* (New York: Doubleday, Anchor Books, 1971), 209–34.

30. Jeffrey, 'Polemarchus and Socrates', makes a similar point, 65–66.

31. Cf. *HMin.* 366b10-c1; *Ly.* 207e-208e. See T. Penner, 'Desire and Power in Socrates: The Argument of *Gorgias* 466a-468e that Orators and Tyrants Have No Power in the City', *Apeiron* 24 (1991): 147–201; R. Weiss, 'Killing, Confiscating, and Banishing at *Gorgias* 466–468', *Ancient Philosophy* 12 (1992): 299–315; K. McTighe, 'Socrates on Desire for the Good and the Involuntariness of Wrongdoing: *Gorgias* 466a-468e', in H. H. Benson, (ed.), *Essays on the Philosophy of Socrates* (Oxford: Oxford University Press, 1992), 263–97.

32. Weiss, 'Killing, Confiscating, and Banishing', makes a similar point, 304, n. 14.

Chapter 4: Ambiguity and Drama

1. The distinction between linguistic and non-linguistic fallacies is not as straightforward as it sounds. In this section, I can do no more than give a bare sketch of

Aristotle's theory of fallacy, and some of its problems. See the introduction of S. G. Schreiber, *Aristotle on False Reasoning: Language and the World in the Sophistical Refutations* (Albany: State University of New York Press, 2003), 1–7, and note 3.

2. Aristotle's first example of homonymy is the *manthanein* equivocation (165b32–34). In an amphiboly, an expression may have more than one meaning, even though none of its components is homonymous, i.e. 'knowing letters' (166a18-22). The term 'amphiboly' is sometimes used by Aristotle loosely to refer to double meaning (*Poetics*, 1461a25-26; *Rh.* 1375b11, 1407a37; *Topics* 160a29). 'Amphiboly' is the standard term for ambiguity used by the Stoics.

3. This particular formulation of Aristotle's classification comes from C. I. Hamblin, *Fallacies* (London: Methuen, 1970), 62–63. I do not follow Forster's translation on many of the names for the fallacies in the Loeb edition. For various discussions of Aristotle's account of ambiguity, see C. Atherton, *The Stoics on Ambiguity* (Cambridge: Cambridge University Press, 1993), 99–109; R. Edlow, *Galen on Language and Ambiguity* (Leiden: E. J. Brill, 1977), 17–31; Hamblin, *Fallacies*, 50–66; W. B. Stanford, *Ambiguity in Greek Literature* (Oxford: Oxford University Press, 1939), 25–55; C. Kirwan, 'Aristotle and the So-called Fallacy of Equivocation', *Philosophical Quarterly* 29 (1979): 35–46; J. P. Anton, 'The Aristotelian Doctrine of *Homonyma* in the *Categories* and its Platonic Antecedents', *Journal of the History of Philosophy* 6 (1969): 315–26; T. H. Irwin, 'Homonymy in Aristotle', *Review of Metaphysics* 34 (1981): 523–44; C. Shields, *Order in Multiplicity: Homonymy in the Philosophy of Aristotle* (Oxford: Oxford University Press, 1999).

4. For a discussion of how the fallacy types would violate one or more of the conditions set down in the definition, see Schreiber, *Aristotle on False Reasoning*, 87–90.

5. Also see Aristotle's point, where a device may be needed: *Topics* 111b32-112a15; cf. *SE* 172b25-28. Aristotle discusses homonymy and gives advice at *Topics* 110a23-110b15, and 148a23-148b22.

6. R. Wardy, *The Birth of Rhetoric: Gorgias, Plato and their Successors* (London and New York: Routledge, 1998), 108–38.

7. Edlow, *Galen on Language and Ambiguity*; 'The Stoics on Ambiguity', *Journal of the History of Philosophy* 13 (1975): 423–35.

8. Diogenes Laertius, *Lives of Eminent Philosophers*, Vol. II, trans. R. D. Hicks (London: Heinemann, 1931), VII.62, p. 171. Cf. Atherton, *The Stoics on Ambiguity*, 133, 212–14; Edlow, *Galen on Language and Ambiguity*, 423–35. A brief definition of ambiguity as 'a word or phrase having two or more meanings' which presumably belonged to the Dogmatists, is given by the skeptic, Sextus Empiricus, in the *Outlines of Pyrrhonism* (2.256, trans. Bury).

9. Atherton, *The Stoics on Ambiguity*, 56–58, 107, 460, 500.

10. Diogenes, *Lives*, VII.46–47, p. 157. Cf. A. A. Long, 'Dialectic and the Stoic Sage', in J. Rist, *The Stoics* (Berkeley: University of California Press, 1978), 101–24.

11. Atherton, *The Stoics on Ambiguity*, 57.

12. Atherton, *The Stoics on Ambiguity*, 58.

13. Atherton, *The Stoics on Ambiguity*, 107.

14. Atherton, *The Stoics on Ambiguity*, 123, as reported by Sextus (*Against the Professors* II.22). She refers to both Galen (94–99) and Alexander of Aphrodisias (122–25) as heavily criticizing the Stoics for assigning their own meaning to terms.

15. Stanford, *Ambiguity in Greek Literature*; Simon Goldhill, *Reading Greek Tragedy* (Cambridge: Cambridge University Press, 1986); and J. P. Vernant and P. Vidal-Naquet, *Myth and Tragedy in Ancient Greece*, trans. Janet Lloyd (New York: Zone Books, 1988).

16. Stanford, *Ambiguity in Greek Literature*, 77.

17. Stanford, *Ambiguity in Greek Literature*, 74.

18. Cf. C. Gill (trans.), *Plato: The Symposium* (London: Penguin Books, 1999), 74.

19. Cf. *Prt.* 337a-c; *Crat.* 384b-c; *La.* 197d; *Chrm.* 163a-b; *Eud.* 277e; *Meno* 75e, 96d.

20. The Greek word '*deinos*' has a wide range of meanings; see *LSJ*, 176–77.

21. Stanford, *Ambiguity in Greek Literature*, 35.

22. Aristotle mentions this type of rhetorical strategy of calling attention to someone's name in argument (*Rh.* 1400b17-30). Socrates makes this move with Polus (*Grg.* 4632-3).

23. Cf. D. Sedley, *Plato's* Cratylus (Cambridge: Cambridge University Press, 2003); C. D. C. Reeve (trans.), *Plato*: Cratylus (Indianapolis: Hackett Publishing Co., 1998).

24. The point I am making here is developed further by J. Gordon, *Turning Toward Philosophy* (University Park: Pennsylvania University State Press, 1999), 113.

25. Euripides, *Bacchae* 968. S. Esposito (trans.), *Euripides: Four Plays. Medea, Hippolytus, Heracles, Bacchae* (Newburyport, MA: Focus Publishing Co., 2002), 246.

26. D. Walton, *Fallacies Arising from Ambiguity* (Dordrecht: Kluwer Academic Publishers, 1996). Walton provides a conversational approach to the fallacies of ambiguity which contrasts with the formalist view.

27. J. Beversluis, *Cross-examining Socrates: A Defense of the Interlocutors in Plato's Early Dialogues* (Cambridge: Cambridge University Press, 2000), 41–42. For a critical review, see C. Gill, 'Speaking Up for Plato's Interlocutors: A Discussion of J. Beversluis, *Cross-examining Socrates*', *Oxford Studies in Ancient Philosophy* 20 (2001): 297–321.

28. Aristotle, *Rh.* II.24.

29. Aristotle, *Rh.* 1419b2-4; cf. *Grg.* 473e.

30. Aristotle talks about the principles of delivery that a speaker should bear in mind and though the 'whole business of rhetoric' is 'concerned with appearances, we must pay attention to the subject of delivery, unworthy though it is, because we cannot do without it' (*Rh.* 1404a2-4).

31. The comedies of Aristophanes and their enormous impact on Plato and his style of writing are discussed by P.A. Vander Waerdt, 'Socrates in the Clouds', in idem (ed.), *The Socratic Movement* (Ithaca: Cornell University Press, 1994), 48–86; M. Lutz, *Socrates' Education to Virtue: Learning the Love of the Noble* (Albany: State University of New York Press, 1998).

32. J. S. Murray, 'Interpreting Plato on Sophistic Claims and the Provenance of the "Socratic Method"', *Phoenix* 48 (1994): 115–34.

33. Aristotle says, 'For what makes the sophist is not the faculty but the moral purpose' (*Rh.* 1355b18-22; cf. *Metaph.* 1004b23-26).

34. Cf. Aristotle's comments on the distinction between eristic and non-eristic sophistry (*SE* 171b21-34).

35. J. Gentzler, 'The Sophistic Cross-examination of Callicles in the *Gorgias*', *Ancient Philosophy* 15 (1995): 17–43; K. McTighe, 'Socrates on Desire for the Good and the Involuntariness of Wrongdoing: *Gorgias* 466a-468e', in H. H. Benson (ed.), *Essays on the Philosophy of Socrates* (Oxford: Oxford University Press, 1992), 263–97.

36. A. W. Nightingale, *Genres in Dialogue: Plato and the Construct of Philosophy* (Cambridge: Cambridge University Press, 1993).

Bibliography

1. Primary Sources

Unless otherwise noted, translations of Plato are taken from The Loeb Classical Library Collection, Vols. I–XII, edited and translated by W. R. M. Lamb, H. Fowler, P. Shorey (London: Heinemann and Cambridge, MA: Harvard University Press). Translations of Aristotle are taken from The Loeb Classical Library Collection, edited and translated by E. S. Forster, J. H. Freese, H. Rackham (London: Heinemann and Cambridge, MA: Harvard University Press). All other Greek texts and translations which I have consulted are listed below.

Aeschylus

The Oresteia. Trans. R. Fagles. London: Penguin Books, 1966.

Aristophanes

The Clouds. Trans. B. B. Rogers. London: Heinemann and Cambridge, MA: Harvard University Press, 1931.
The Frogs. Trans. B. B. Rogers. London: Heinemann and Cambridge, MA: Harvard University Press, 1924.
The Clouds, The Birds, Lysistrata, The Frogs. Trans. W. Arrowsmith, R. Lattimore, D. Parker. London: Meridian, Penguin Books, 1994.

Aristotle

The Complete Works of Aristotle: The Revised Oxford Translation. 2 volumes. Ed. J. Barnes. Princeton: Princeton University Press, 1981.

Diogenes Laertius

Lives of Eminent Philosophers. Vols I-II. Trans. R. D. Hicks. London: Heinemann and Cambridge, MA: Harvard University Press, 1931.

Euripides

Bacchae. Trans. A. S. Way. London: Heinemann and Cambridge, MA: Harvard University Press, 1931.

Euripides: Four Plays. Medea, Hippolytus, Heracles, Bacchae. Trans. A. J. Podlecki, M. R. Halleran, S. Esposito. Newburyport, MA: Focus Publishing Co., 2002.

Gorgias

Encomium of Helen. Trans. D. M. MacDowell. Bristol: Bristol Classical Press, 1982.

Homer

The Iliad. Trans. R. Fagles. London: Penguin Books, 1990.
The Odyssey. Trans. E. V. Rieu. London: Penguin Books, 2003.

Plato

Charmides. Trans. T. G. Tuckey. Cambridge: Cambridge University Press, 1951.

Clitophon. Trans. S. R. Slings. Cambridge: Cambridge University Press, 1999.

Cratylus. Trans. C. D. C. Reeve. Indianapolis: Hackett Publishing Co., 1998.

Euthydemus. Trans. R. K. Sprague. Hackett Publishing Co., 1993.

Euthyphro, Apology of Socrates, Crito. Ed. J. Burnet. Oxford: Oxford University Press, 2002.

Five Dialogues: Apology, Crito, Euthyphro, Meno, Phaedo. Trans. G. M. A. Grube. Indianapolis: Hackett Publishing Co., 1981.

Gorgias. Trans. E. R. Dodds. Oxford: Clarendon Press, 2002 [1959].

Gorgias. Trans. D. Zeyl. Indianapolis: Hackett Publishing Co., 1987.

Ion. Trans. R. E. Allen. *The Dialogues of Plato*. New Haven and London: Yale University Press, 1984.

Laches and *Charmides*. Trans. R. K. Sprague. Indianapolis: Hackett Publishing Co., 1992.

Phaedo. Ed. J. Burnet. Oxford: Oxford University Press, 1989.

Philebus. Trans. R. Waterfield. London: Penguin Books, 1982.

Protagoras. Trans. S. Lombardo and K. Bell. Indianapolis: Hackett Publishing Co., 1992.

Republic Book I. Trans. D. J. Allan. London: Methuen, 1953.

Republic. Trans. G. M. A. Grube, rev. C. D. C. Reeve. Indianapolis: Hackett Publishing Co., 1992.

Symposium. Trans. C. Gill. London: Penguin Books, 1999.

Theaetetus. Trans. R. Waterfield. London: Penguin Books, 1987.

Theaetetus. Trans. M. J. Levett. Indianapolis: Hackett Publishing Co., 1992.

Sextus Empiricus

Against the Professors. Trans. R. G. Bury. London: Heinemann and Cambridge, MA: Harvard University Press, 1933.
Outlines of Pyrrhonism. Trans. R. G. Bury. London: Heinemann and Cambridge, MA: Harvard University Press, 1933.

Sophocles

Ajax, Electra, Trachiniae, Philoctetes. Trans. F. Storr. London: Heinemann and Cambridge, MA: Harvard University Press, 1913.
Four Dramas of Maturity: Aias, Antigone, Young Women of Trachis, Oidipous the King. Trans. M. Ewans, G. Ley, G. McCart. Guernsey: Guernsey Press Co., 1999.

Thucydides

History of the Peloponnesian War. Trans. R. Warner. London: Penguin Books, 1972.

Xenophon

Conversation of Socrates. Trans. H. Tredennick and R. Waterfield. London: Penguin Books, 1990.

2. Secondary Sources

Adkins, A. W. H., *Moral Values and Political Behaviour in Ancient Greece.* New York: Norton, 1972.
—— *Merit and Responsibility: A Study in Greek Values.* Oxford: Clarendon Press, 1960.
Ahbel-Rappe, S. and R. Kamtekar (eds), *A Companion to Socrates.* Oxford: Blackwell, 2006.
Annas, J., *An Introduction to Plato's Republic.* New York: Oxford University Press, 1981.
Anton, J. P., 'The Aristotelian Doctrine of *Homonyma* in the *Categories* and its Platonic Antecedents'. *Journal of the History of Philosophy* 6 (1969): 315–26.
Atherton C., *The Stoics on Ambiguity.* Cambridge: Cambridge University Press, 1993.
Bailly, J., 'What You Say, What You Believe, and What You Mean'. *Ancient Philosophy* 19 (1999): 65–76.
Bensen, R., *Socratic Method and Self-knowledge in Plato's Early Dialogues.* Ann Arbor: University Microfilms Inc., 1999.
Benson, H. H., *Socratic Wisdom: The Model of Knowledge in Plato's Early Dialogues.* Oxford: Oxford University Press, 2000.
Beversluis, J., *Cross-examining Socrates: A Defense of the Interlocutors in Plato's Early Dialogues.* Cambridge: Cambridge University Press, 2000.

Blondell, R., *The Play of Character in Plato's Dialogues*. Cambridge: Cambridge University Press, 2002.

Blundell, M. W., *Helping Friends and Harming Enemies: A Study in Sophocles and Greek Ethics*. Cambridge: Cambridge University Press, 1989.

Bolton, R., 'Aristotle's Account of Socratic Elenchus'. *Oxford Studies in Ancient Philosophy* 11 (1993): 121–52.

Brickhouse, T. and N. D. Smith *Socrates on Trial*. Princeton: Princeton University Press, 1989.

—— *Plato's Socrates*. Oxford: Oxford University Press, 1994.

Burnyeat, M., 'Virtues in Action', in G. Vlastos (ed.), *Plato: A Collection of Critical Essays*. New York: Doubleday, Anchor Books, 1971, 209–34.

—— 'Fathers and Sons in Plato's *Republic* and *Philebus*'. *Classical Quarterly* 54.1 (2004): 80–87.

Cairns, D. L., Aidōs: *The Psychology and Ethics of Honour and Shame in Ancient Greek Literature*. Oxford: Clarendon Press, 1993.

Chance, T., *Plato's* Euthydemus: *Analysis of What Is and Is Not Philosophy*. Berkeley: University of California Press, 1992.

Clay, D., 'The Origins of the Socratic Dialogue', in P. Vander Waerdt (ed.), *The Socratic Movement*. Ithaca: Cornell University Press, 1994, 23–47.

Cohen, M. H., 'The aporias in Plato's Early Dialogues'. *Journal of the History of Ideas* 23.3 (1962): 163–74.

—— *Plato's Use of Ambiguity and Deliberate Fallacy: An Interpretation of the Implicit Doctrines of the 'Charmides' and 'Lysis'*. Ph.D. dissertation, Columbia University: Ann Arbor: University Microfilms Inc., 1963.

Collard, C., 'Formal Debates in Euripides' Drama'. *Greece and Rome* 22 (1975): 58–71.

Cross, R. C. and A. D. Woozley *Plato's Republic: A Philosophical Commentary*. London: Macmillan, 1964.

Desjardins, R., 'Why Dialogues? Plato's Serious Play', in C. Griswold (ed.), *Platonic Writings, Platonic Readings*. London and New York: Routledge, 1988, 110–25.

Dodds, E. R., *Greeks and the Irrational*. Berkeley and Los Angeles: University of California Press, 1951.

Dover, K. J., *Greek Popular Morality in the Time of Plato and Aristotle*. Indianapolis: Hackett Publishing Co., 1994 [Oxford: Blackwell, 1974].

Edlow, R. B., 'The Stoics on Ambiguity'. *Journal of the History of Philosophy* 13 (1975): 423–35.

—— *Galen on Language and Ambiguity*. Leiden: Brill, 1977.

Friedländer, P., *Plato*. Vol. I. Hans Meyerhoff (trans.). London: Pantheon Books, 1964.

Gadamer, H. G., *Dialogue and Dialectic: Eight Hermeneutical Studies on Plato*. Trans. P. C. Smith. New Haven and London: Yale University Press, 1980.

—— *Plato's Dialectical Ethics: Phenomenological Interpretations Relating to the* Philebus. Trans. R. M. Wallace. New Haven and London: Yale University Press, 1983.

Gagarin, M., *Antiphon the Athenian*. Austin: University of Texas Press, 2002.

Gentzler, J., 'The Sophistic Cross-examination of Callicles in the *Gorgias*'. *Ancient Philosophy* 15 (1995): 17–43.

Gifford, M., 'Dramatic Dialectic in *Republic* Book I'. *Oxford Studies in Ancient Philosophy* 20 (2001): 35–106.

Gill, C., 'Speaking Up for Plato's Interlocutors: A Discussion of J. Beversluis, *Cross-examining Socrates*'. *Oxford Studies in Ancient Philosophy* 20 (2001): 297–321.

Goldhill, S., *Reading Greek Tragedy*. Cambridge: Cambridge University Press, 1986.

Gonzalez, F. J., *The Third Way: New Dimensions in Platonic Studies*. Lanham, MD: Rowman & Littlefield, 1995.

—— *Dialectic and Dialogue: Plato's Practice of Philosophical Inquiry*. Evanston: Northwestern University Press, 1998.

Gordon, J., *Turning Toward Philosophy: Literary Device and Dramatic Structure in Plato's Dialogues*. University Park: Pennsylvania State University Press, 1999.

Grote, G., *Plato and Other Companions of Sokrates*. 3 vols. Trans. J. Murray. London: J. Murray, 1865.

Guthrie, W. K. C., *A History of Greek Philosophy, Plato: The Man and His Dialogues: The Earlier Period*. Vol. IV. Cambridge: Cambridge University Press, 1978.

Hamblin, C. I., *Fallacies*. London: Methuen, 1970.

Hawtrey, R. S. W., *Commentary on Plato's* Euthydemus. Philadelphia: American Philosophical Society, 1981.

Hornblower, S. and A. Spawforth *The Oxford Classical Dictionary*. 3rd ed. Oxford: Oxford University Press, 2003.

Irwin, T. H., *Plato's Moral Theory*. Oxford: Clarendon Press, 1977.

—— 'Homonymy in Aristotle'. *Review of Metaphysics* 34 (1981): 523–44.

—— 'Coercion and Objectivity in Plato's Dialectic'. *Revue de Internationale* 40 (1986): 49–74.

—— 'Socratic Puzzles'. *Oxford Studies in Ancient Philosophy* 10 (1992): 241–66.

—— *Plato's Ethics*. Oxford: Oxford University Press, 1995.

Jeffrey, A., 'Polemarchus and Socrates on Justice and Harm'. *Phronesis* 24 (1979): 54–69.

Kahn, C., 'Drama and Dialectic in Plato's *Gorgias*'. *Oxford Studies in Ancient Philosophy* 1 (1983): 75–121.

—— *Plato and the Socratic Dialogue: The Philosophical Use of a Literary Form*. Cambridge: Cambridge University Press, 1996.

Kennedy, G. A. (ed.), *The Cambridge History of Literary Criticism*. Vol. I. Cambridge: Cambridge University Press.

Kerferd, G. B., *The Sophistic Movement*. Cambridge: Cambridge University Press, 1981.

Kierkegaard, S., *The Concept of Irony with Continual Reference to Socrates*. H. V. Hong and E. H. Hong (eds and trans.). Princeton: Princeton University Press, 1989.

Kirwan, C., 'Aristotle and the So-called Fallacy of Equivocation'. *Philosophical Quarterly* 29 (1979): 35–46.

Klein, S. 'The Value of *Endoxa* in Ethical Argument'. *History of Philosophical Quarterly* 9.2 (1992): 141–57.

Klosko, G., 'Toward a Consistent Interpretation of the *Protagoras*'. *Archiv für Geschichte der Philosophie* 61 (1975): 125–42.

—— 'Criteria of Fallacy and Sophistry for Use in the Analysis of Plato's Dialogues'. *Classical Quarterly* 33 (1983): 363–74.

—— 'Plato and the Morality of Fallacy'. *American Journal of Philology* 108 (1987): 616–26.

Kooij, J., *Ambiguity in Natural Language*. Amsterdam: North-Holland Publishing, 1971.

Kraut, R., 'Comments on Gregory Vlastos, "The Socratic Elenchus" '. *Oxford Studies in Ancient Philosophy* 1 (1983): 59–70.

—— 'Critical Review: Brickhouse and Smith's *Plato's Socrates*', Ancient Philosophy 15 (1995): 619–45.

Lear, J., *Open Minded: Working Out the Logic of the Soul*. Harvard: Harvard University Press, 1998.

Liddell, H. G. and R. A. Scott, *Greek-English Lexicon*. Oxford: Oxford University Press, 1985.

Lloyd, G. E. R., *Magic, Reason, and Experience: Studies in the Origins and Development of Greek Science*. Indianapolis: Hackett Publishing Co., 1979.

Long, A. A., 'Dialectic and the Stoic Sage', in J. Rist, *The Stoics*. Berkeley: University of California Press, 1978, 101–24.

—— 'Plato's Apologies and Socrates in the *Theaetetus*', in J. Gentzler (ed.), *Method in Ancient Philosophy*. Oxford: Clarendon Press, 1998, 113–36.

Lutz, M., *Socrates' Education to Virtue: Learning the Love of the Noble*. Albany: State University of New York Press, 1998.

McKim, R., 'Shame and Truth in Plato's *Gorgias*', in C. Griswold (ed.), *Platonic Writings, Platonic Readings*. New York: Routledge, 1988, 34–48.

McPherran, M., 'Socratic Piety in the *Euthyphro*', in H. H. Benson (ed.), *Essays on the Philosophy of Socrates*. Oxford: Oxford University Press, 1992, 220–41.

—— *The Religion of Socrates*. University Park: Pennsylvania State University Press, 1996.

McTighe, K. , 'Socrates on Desire for the Good and the Involuntariness of Wrongdoing: *Gorgias* 466a-468e', in H. H. Benson (ed.), *Essays on the Philosophy of Socrates*. Oxford: Oxford University Press, 1992, 263–97.

Morrison, J. S., *Antiphon*, in R. K. Sprague (ed.), *The Older Sophists*. Columbia: University of South Carolina Press, 1972, 106–240.

Murray, J. S., 'Interpreting Plato on Sophistic Claims and the Provenance of the "Socratic Method" '. *Phoenix*, 48 (1994): 115–34.

Nails, D., 'Problems with Vlastos's Platonic Developmentalism'. *Ancient Philosophy* 13 (1993): 273–91.

—— *The People of Plato: A Prosopography of Plato and Other Socratics*. Indianapolis: Hackett Publishing Co., 2002.

Nietzsche, F., *Twilight of the Idols Or, How to Philosophize with a Hammer*. Trans. R. Polt. Indianapolis: Hackett Publishing Co., 1997.

Nightingale, A. W., *Genres in Dialogue: Plato and the Construct of Philosophy*. Cambridge: Cambridge University Press, 1993.

Ostenfeld, E., 'Socratic Argumentation Strategies and Aristotle's *Topics* and *Sophistical Refutations*'. *Methexis* 9 (1996): 43–57.

Patterson, R., 'The Platonic Art of Comedy and Tragedy'. *Philosophy and Literature* 6 (1982): 76–93.

Penner, T., 'Desire and Power in Socrates: The Argument of *Gorgias* 466a-468e that Orators and Tyrants Have No Power in the City'. *Apeiron* 24 (1991): 147–201.

Polansky, R., 'Professor Vlastos's Analysis of Socratic Elenchus'. *Oxford Studies in Ancient Philosophy* 3 (1985): 247–59.

Press, G., 'The State of the Question in the Study of Plato'. *Southern Journal of Philosophy* 34 (1996): 507–32 (N. D. Smith, 1998).

—— *Who Speaks for Plato?: Studies in Platonic Anonymity.* Lanham, MD: Rowman & Littlefield, 2000.

Robinson, R., 'Ambiguity', *Mind* 50 (1942): 140–55.

—— *Plato's Earlier Dialectic.* Oxford: Clarendon Press, 1953.

Roochnik, D., 'Socrates' Use of the Techne Analogy'. *Journal of the History of Philosophy* 24 (1986): 295–310.

—— *Of Art and Wisdom: Plato's Understanding of Techne.* University Park: Pennsylvania State University Press, 1996.

Rutherford, R. B., *The Art of Plato: Ten Essays in Platonic Interpretation.* Cambridge, MA: Harvard University Press, 1995.

Santas, G., *Socrates: Philosophy in Plato's Early Dialogues.* London: Routledge & Kegan Paul, 1979.

Schmid, W. T., 'Socrates' Practice of Elenchus in the *Charmides*'. *Ancient Philosophy* 1 (1981): 141–47.

Schreiber, S. G., *Aristotle on False Reasoning: Language and the World in the Sophistical Refutations.* Albany: State University of New York Press, 2003.

Scott, G. A., *Plato's Socrates as Educator.* Albany: State University of New York Press, 2000.

Scott, G. A. (ed.), *Does Socrates Have a Method? Rethinking the* Elenchus *in Plato's Dialogues and Beyond.* University Park: Pennsylvania State University Press, 2002.

Sedley, D., *Plato's* Cratylus. Cambridge: Cambridge University Press, 2003.

Seeskin, K., 'Socratic Philosophy and the Dialogue Form', *Philosophy and Literature* 8 (1984): 181–93.

Shields, C., *Order in Multiplicity: Homonymy in the Philosophy of Aristotle.* Oxford: Oxford University Press, 1999.

Sinaiko, H. L., *Love, Knowledge, and Discourse in Plato: Dialogue and Dialectic in Phaedrus, Republic, Parmenides.* Chicago: University of Chicago Press, 1965.

Smith, N. D. (ed.), *Plato: Critical Assessments*, vol. I. New York: Routledge, 1998.

Sprague, R. K., *Plato's Use of Fallacy: A Study of the* Euthydemus *and Some Other Dialogues.* London: Routledge & Kegan Paul, 1962.

—— 'Logic and Literary Form in Plato'. *The Personalist* 48 (1967): 560–72.

—— 'Plato's Sophistry'. *The Aristotelian Society*, Supp., Vol. 51 (1977): 45–61.

Stanford, W. B., *Ambiguity in Greek Literature.* Oxford: Oxford University Press, 1939.

Stewart, M. A., 'Plato's Sophistry'. *The Aristotelian Society*, Supp., 51 (1977): 21–44.

Tarrant, D., 'Plato as Dramatist'. *Journal of Hellenic Studies* 25 (1955): 82–89.

Teloh, H., *Socratic Education in Plato's Early Dialogues.* Notre Dame: University of Notre Dame Press, 1986.

Thayer, H. S., 'Plato: The Theory and Language of Function', in A. Sesonske (ed.), *Plato's* Republic: *Interpretation and Criticism*. Belmont: Wadsworth Publishing Co., 1966, 21–39.

Vander Waerdt, P. A., 'Socrates in the Clouds', in idem (ed.) *The Socratic Movement*, 48–86. Ithaca: Cornell University Press, 1994.

Vernant J. P. and Vidal-Naquet, P., *Myth and Tragedy in Ancient Greece*. Trans. Janet Lloyd. New York: Zone Books, 1988.

Vlastos, G., 'Was Polus Refuted?'. *American Journal of Philology* 88 (1967): 454–60.

—— 'The Socratic Elenchus'. *Oxford Studies in Ancient Philosophy* 1 (1983): 27–58.

—— *Socrates: Ironist, and Moral Philosopher*. Ithaca: Cornell University Press,1991.

—— *Socratic Studies*. M. Burnyeat (ed.). Cambridge: Cambridge University Press, 1994.

Walton, D., *Fallacies Arising from Ambiguity*. Dordrecht: Kluwer Academic Publishers, 1996.

Wardy, R., *The Birth of Rhetoric: Gorgias, Plato and their Successors*. London and New York: Routledge, 1998.

Weingartner, R. H., *The Unity of the Platonic Dialogue*. Indianapolis: Bobbs-Merrill, 1973.

Weiss, R. 'Killing, Confiscating, and Banishing at *Gorgias* 466–468.' *Ancient Philosophy* 12 (1992): 299–315.

Williams, B., *Shame and Necessity*. Berkeley and Los Angeles: University of California Press, 1993.

Wolz, H., 'Philosophy as Drama: An Approach to Plato's Dialogues'. *International Philosophical Quarterly* 3 (1963): 236–70.

Woodruff, P., 'Socrates and the Irrational', in N. D. Smith and P. Woodruff (eds), *Reason and Religion in Socratic Philosophy*. Oxford: Oxford University Press, 2000, 130–50.

Zembaty, J., 'Socrates' Perplexity in Plato's *Hippias Minor*', in J. Anton and A. Preus (eds), *Essays in Greek Philosophy* III. Albany: State University of New York Press, 1989, 51–70.

Index

B395 .B43 2007

Bensen Cain, Rebecca,

The Socratic method :
 Plato's use of
      c2007.

0 1341 1091301 6

RECEIVED

JUL 0 8 2008

GUELPH HUMBER LIBRARY
205 Humber College Blvd
Toronto, ON M9W 5L7